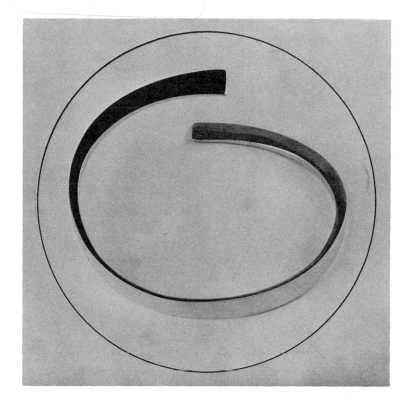

STEP-BY-STEP

jewelry

A Complete Introduction to the Craft of Jewelry

By Thomas Gentille

Conceived and edited by
William and Shirley Sayles

 **GOLDEN PRESS · NEW YORK**

WESTERN PUBLISHING COMPANY, INC.
Racine, Wisconsin

To Mary B. Bishop and Francis Merritt

Library of Congress Catalog Card Number: 67-21708
© *Copyright 1968 by Western Publishing Company, Inc. All rights reserved, including rights of reproduction and use in any form or by any means, including the making of copies by any photo process, or by any electronic or mechanical device, printed or written or oral, or recording for sound or visual reproduction or for use in any knowledge retrieval system or device, unless permission in writing is obtained from the copyright proprietor. Produced in the U.S.A. by Western Publishing Company, Inc. Published by Golden Press, New York. N.Y.*

GOLDEN PRESS ® *is a trademark of Western Publishing Company, Inc.*

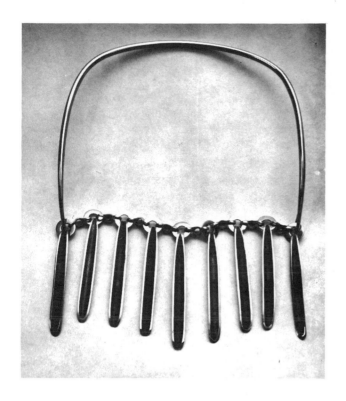

contents

PROJECTS:

1 Sawed Pin 40
2 Sawed Pin with Back Plate 42
3 Fused Pin 44
4 Filed Pin 46
5 Simple Ring 48
6 Split Ring 51
7 Pendant 52
8 Silver Chains 54
9 Silver Comb 56
10 Gold Pin with Stone 58

ADVANCED TECHNIQUES:

Forging 60
Enameling 66
Casting 70
Granulation 76
Electroforming 78
Combined Methods 82

LAPIDARY 86
FOUND OBJECT JEWELRY 90
GLOSSARY 94
SUPPLIERS 95
BIBLIOGRAPHY 95
SCHOOLS 96

INTRODUCTION 4
TYPES OF JEWELRY 12
TOOLS AND MATERIALS 16
SAFETY 19
METALS 20
WORKSHOP 21

BASIC PROCESSES:

Sawing 22
Filing 23
Soldering 24
Buffing 28

OXIDIZING 30
BEZELS 31
ADDITIONAL INFORMATION 32
SURFACE TREATMENTS 34
DESIGN PORTFOLIO 36

acknowledgments

In the course of preparing this book many craftsmen were asked for photographic examples of their work, and their cooperation was very gratifying—thanks go to them and to Craft Horizons, to the American Craftsmen's Council, and to the Cleveland Museum of Art for lending photographic material from their collections.
Among those who have assisted in the preparation of this book, special thanks are due to:

Hal Halverstadt, *Consultant*
Sandra Zimmerman, *Research, A.C.C.*
Betty MacDonald, *Design*
Louis Mervar, *Photography*
Paul Compare, *Artist*

introduction

Elizabeth, who is ten, said "jewelry is rings and stuff" and so it is. I took her by the hand, and we walked out into the yard and strung some oak leaves onto a yellow string and made a necklace.

Making jewelry is not quite that simple, but its basic processes are few and, with application, can be learned quickly. It is a craft that can be easily practiced at home; it does not require a lot of space, in fact, the work area can be rather compact and just allow enough room for a workbench and easy maneuverability. The tools are nominal in price, can last for years and, since only a small number are necessary—you add more as you need them—do not represent any great investment. Nearly all of them are well made, and buying the best quality is always the wisest choice.

The materials, with the exception of gold and precious stones, are also nominal in cost and easy to come by, no matter where you live. The additional cost of gold should not discourage you from using it, however. It is the most malleable and ductile of materials—it responds more than any other metal to being hammered or rolled and to being drawn into fine wire. Some craftsmen feel that they work best in gold and find it beautiful in all stages. The other metals used throughout this book are silver, brass, and copper. Silver for malleability and ductility is second only to gold and is superb when polished. When you begin working with the metals, you will quickly find your own preference.

Jewelry is a metalworking craft. The jeweler is actually a goldsmith or a silversmith—if he works mainly with either metal—or a metalsmith, if he works with others as well.

The singular purpose of jewelry is to adorn the human form: to decorate the finger, to grace the neck, to enhance the ear. To these ends it places no limits on your imagination. With concern only for the demands of function—weight and balance—you can use such materials as silver, gold, platinum, bronze, brass, copper, wood, bone, and ivory, singly or in combination. You can incorporate color with precious or semiprecious stones, or by enameling. Or you can use a handsome beach pebble, or include some interesting old beads or even adapt a piece of antique jewelry to a contemporary setting. As in all areas of the arts, often the most fascinating works combine the everyday or found object with precious or semiprecious materials.

Whether you are interested in jewelry as an avocation or whether you are a student with serious aspirations, this book is designed to start

Figure headdress in gold from Colombia (called Tunjo). Courtesy of The Cleveland Museum of Art.

Swedish bridal crown, 17th century gilt brass, bronze, and silver with rock crystals. Courtesy of The Cleveland Museum of Art.

you on your way as surely and simply as possible. The section of the book containing the basic processes should be read carefully, since it is with these that you will be able to produce an unlimited variety of work. You need never go beyond these simple processes to produce beautiful pieces, but for the times when you would like to, there are surface treatments, such as etching, engraving, repoussé, or chasing. Also presented is information on stones and how to mount them. Many of the advanced jewelry techniques are included to familiarize you with yet another dimension of jewelry—the different techniques of enameling, "lost wax" casting, forging, and an introduction to granulation and electroforming. Casting is one technique that requires additional equipment and work space, but it is one of the most exciting approaches to the making of jewelry.

The basic processes, together with a few simple tools, will enable you to make the jewelry offered in ten projects. These projects have step-by-step directions with diagrams and progress in logical sequence from a simple sawed pin to more complex pieces such as a pendant with mixed metals and a gold pin with stone. Even though the projects have instructions on how to make a particular piece of jewelry, they are intended as starting points for your own ideas. Once you are more experienced, you will be able to vary the designs as you wish. In all instances, a handsome piece can be developed that will give pleasure in the making and in the wearing as well.

Throughout the book there are photographs chosen for their qualities of design and craftsmanship. They are here not only to show what may be accomplished, but also to present pieces that are worth analyzing for their construction and that will stimulate ideas.

Also well worth studying is the jewelry of other cultures, including the Egyptian, Greek, Roman, and Etruscan, which can be seen in our great museums. The early Egyptians created work of wonderful simplicity, beating gold nuggets into sheets and hammering the thin gleaming metal into the most graceful of shapes. Still later the Greeks and Etruscans formed notable pieces designed with tiny granules of gold, sometimes layer upon layer, in the intricate process known as granulation. Some examples are included here and throughout the book, not only of these cultures but of others as well.

Many people feel lost when they are first confronted with the problem of design. Trips to museums, as mentioned, studying photographs in magazines, in books, and in all, becoming aware of the literally thousands of patterns that surround you every day will be of help. Nature, as any craftsman will tell you, is the greatest of all sources of reference. Look, for example, at how the veins in a leaf are patterned, or the way fern shoots curl, the turn of a petal, or the form of leafless branches in the winter. Also there are the geometric and abstract patterns within your home. Eventually so many ideas will present themselves that the question is no longer of what to do, but which of the many to do first.

It may be a further help to draw an entire page of ideas, sketching whatever design forms come to mind, not with the intent of using them immediately, although you could select one or two to develop, but to put aside and refer to at a later time. A drawing you do today might not excite you, but in a couple of weeks it may be just the one to lead you to the idea that is exactly the one you are looking for. Drawing, then, is a starting point. Ideas also come as you are working on a piece of jewelry, and, before long, you may find that there are more ideas than there is time to develop them.

Another important point is the shape of the piece: will it be a geometric shape of flat sheet metal, or an abstract one of twisted wires, or even something different? Whatever it will be should be determined at the start. It can then be modified, developed further, and perhaps made into a string of like shapes for a necklace or a bracelet. Sometimes, even the shape of a stone you intend using will suggest the design.

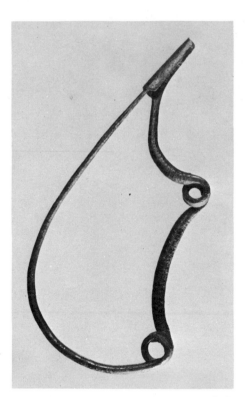

Bronze fibula, Italy 9th–8th century B.C. from The Newark Museum Collection. Photograph by Ferdinand Boesch.

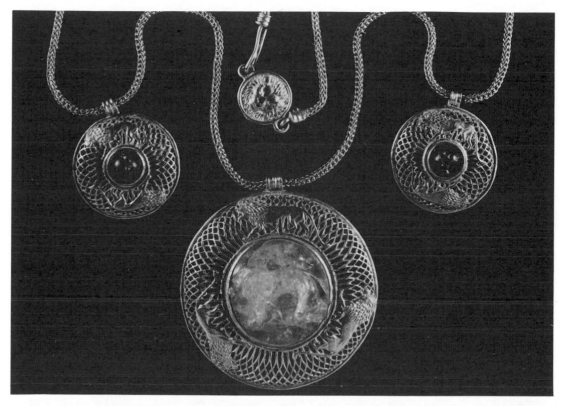

(Top) Gold necklace with stones in three pendant medallions, Egypt, 3rd–2nd century B.C. Courtesy of The Cleveland Museum of Art. (Bottom) Gold necklace from Ghana. Courtesy of The Museum of Primitive Art. Photograph by Charles Uht.

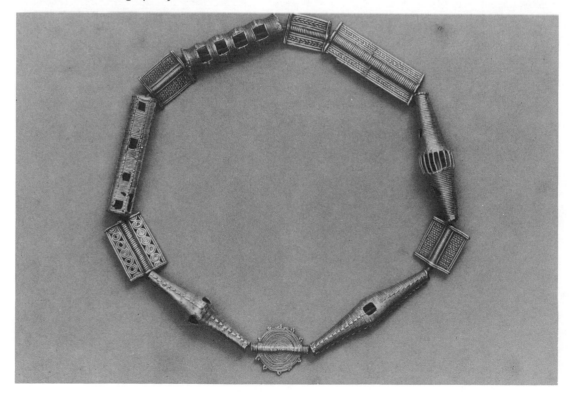

Keep in mind when designing jewelry that it is meant to be worn, and, therefore sharp points should be avoided. The piece should not jab or tear, and a pin should not be so heavy that it will pull or stretch fabrics.

When we think of jewelry, our traditional forms of adornment come to mind: the ring, the bracelet, the cuff link, the tie bar, the belt buckle. Today these items are nearly always made of precious or non-precious metals: silver, platinum, brass, or copper, to name just a few. And, as often as not, gem stones are set into the metal.

At the turn of the century, many other materials and types of ornaments were in common use. The Victorians made jewelry incorporating hair and crystal; brooches and medallions were made to hold locks of hair of someone dear or someone departed. Queen Victoria even had her children's baby teeth mounted in a bracelet. And, this was the period when beads were very much in vogue and were used in many items from neck bands to ornamental fans. Men took pleasure and pride in their pocket watches, some of which were heavily and beautifully engraved. They were held in place with ornate watch fobs and chains made of metal and sometimes of braided fiber.

Each culture produced its own forms and derived its designs from its

Gold mask, embossed, Mochica culture, Peru 400–1000 A.D. Courtesy of The Cleveland Museum of Art.

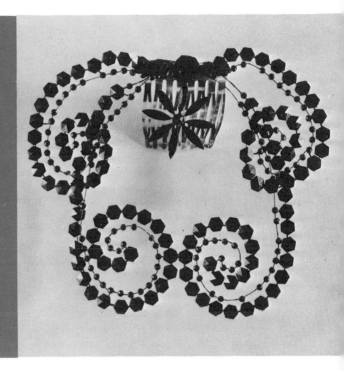

Hair ornament of wired jet beads, American, ca. 1890. Courtesy of The Brooklyn Museum. Photograph by Ferdinand Boesch.

Steel armor of George Clifford, third Earl of Cumberland, K.G. (1558–1605). Courtesy of The Metropolitan Museum of Art.

(Above) Pendant with pelican (the three small subsidiary pendants with pearls, although of the period, were added later.) Enameled gold with rubies, pearls, and emeralds. Germany, ca. 1600. Courtesy of The Cleveland Museum of Art.

(Left) Hat jewel "Adoration of the Kings," France 1540. Courtesy of The Cleveland Museum of Art.

(Opposite page) Contemporary pin of white gold, onyx, jade, and coral by Margaret de Patta. Courtesy of the American Craftsmen's Council. Photograph by Ferdinand Boesch.

needs and surroundings. In ancient Greece and Rome, for example, jewelry had in many instances highly practical considerations and such items as fibula and other special ornaments were constructed to hold garments together. Certain jewelry was also worn to indicate who the distinguished people were, such as the Roman senators and those of certain important family descent.

One of the most frequently worn ornaments in classical antiquity was the seal ring. These rings were used to sign and to authenticate documents and to mark property. Although purely utilitarian in purpose, the examples that we have of those periods are nearly always beautiful and of excellent craftsmanship.

During medieval times, it was the church that was the inspiration for creative efforts and also the recipient of finished works of jewelry. The many magnificent suits of armor for the knighthood were made not only to outfit the man, but his horse as well. The armored suits were highly adorned, generally engraved, and sometimes inlaid with precious and nonprecious metals.

Forms of ornaments and materials used are really only limited by the imagination. Since the beginnings of time, man made his jewelry from the objects that have surrounded him, and today tribal peoples use those selfsame materials—shells, bone, wood, seeds, and feathers, all in a variety of colors, some of muted subtlety, others of rich brilliance.

At the conclusion of the book is a glossary of terms for easy reference, a bibliography, a list of suppliers for tools and materials, and one for schools throughout the country that specialize in jewelry workshops.

It is exciting to think that even with this rich past, there are still further fancies to be contemplated and developed by the craftsmen of today.

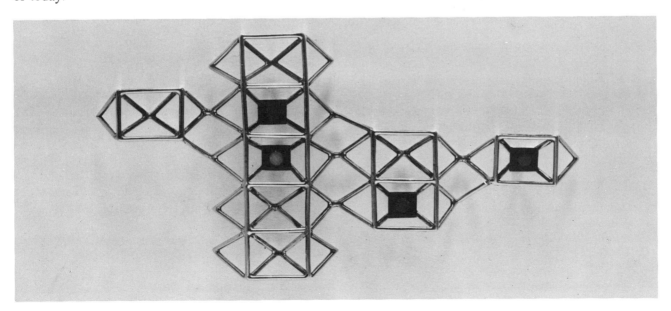

Courtesy of Madeline Green

Courtesy of Craft Horizons

forging

Forging utilizes the malleable quality of metal which allows it to be hammered into various shapes. One of the advantages of this technique is the spring tension created by the hardening of the metal. Such tension can be used to spring a forged bracelet together or to hold earrings or a necklace in place, thus eliminating the need for catches or clasps.

During forging, the metal is placed on a steel block or on smooth steel forms called stakes and, with the use of special hammers, is bent or stretched to shape.

While entire pieces of jewelry can be made by the forging technique alone, small shapes can also be forged and added to shapes made by other techniques.

Forging can be used to form many hollow shapes not only for jewelry but for hollowware as well, which includes teapots, bowls, and spoons.

The gold pin above by Alexander Calder illustrates the direct simplicity that can be achieved in forging.

For this technique see pages 60–65.

enameling

In enameling, finely ground powdered glass is fused onto a metal base. Three of the enameling methods are discussed in this book.

In *cloisonné,* thin partitions, or cloisons, of flat wire bent to shape are soldered to or are placed on a backplate. They are filled with enamels and fired.

In *plique-à-jour* the cloisons are placed on mica which is removed after the firing has taken place. Transparent enamels are generally used and when light passes through them, they resemble stained glass. This technique can be successfully applied to hair ornaments, pendants, earrings, or to any piece through which light is allowed to pass.

In *champlevé,* or inlaid enameling, hollows are punched or cut into the metal to form cells which are inlaid with enamels, either transparent or opaque.

The sterling silver hinged box above, "Clam Shell" by Mary Kretsinger, is an example of cloisonné.

For this technique see pages 66–69.

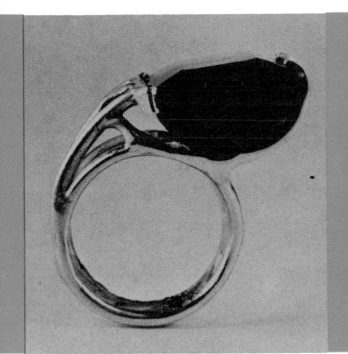

Photograph by Ferdinand Boesch

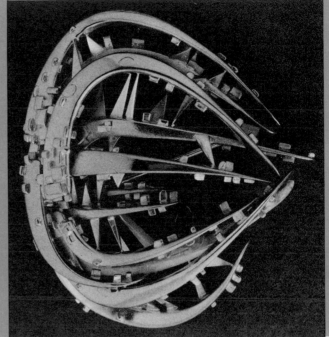

Courtesy of Craft Horizons

casting

In classic casting, the piece of work, usually of wax, is covered with a plaster, clay-like mixture called investment. The wax is then melted out or lost leaving a hollow into which molten metal is poured. This is the technique referred to as "lost wax."

Recently materials such as wood, cloth, and weed pods have been used instead of wax as forms to be burned out. Also special, fine sand can be packed around stryofoam or paper models and frozen with CO_2. Since these materials vaporize upon contact with molten metal, firing a kiln is eliminated.

In sand casting, an early method, metal is poured into a depression scooped out of fine sand. Sharp detail is difficult to achieve here and somewhat more can be given to forms hollowed out of cuttle bone.

The ring above by the author was first made of wax then cast in yellow gold. The stone, a purple amethyst, is positioned so that it rests between the ring finger and the one adjacent.

For this technique see pages 70–75.

granulation

Granulation is the art of fastening tiny granules, usually of gold, onto the surface of a piece of work without the use of solder.

This delicate and sophisticated gold work was at its height during Hellenistic times and was fashioned also by the early craftsmen of Rome and Assyria. Today a few craftsmen are successfully rediscovering the granulation process, and several possible ways of working it have been advanced.

The small spherical granules are not difficult to make and the stages leading up to fusing them onto the gold base work are not complicated.

Fastening the granules to the metal takes place when they are both heated and when the molecules of both surfaces interchange and lock together.

The gold pin above, by John Paul Miller, is constructed of forged shapes and granulation. Here the granules are not in the traditional round forms.

For this technique see pages 76–77.

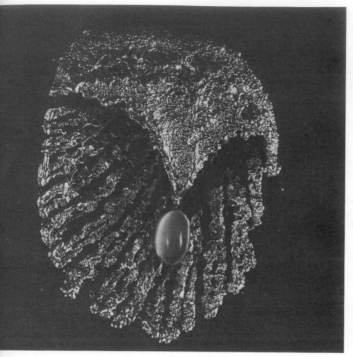

Courtesy of Stanley Lechtzin

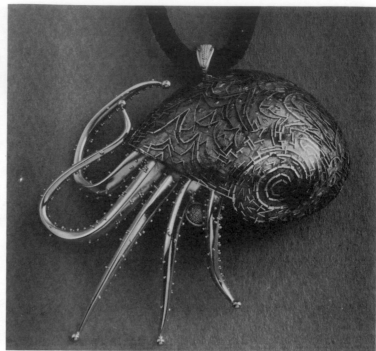

Courtesy of John Paul Miller

electroforming

Electroforming, a unique and recent method of forming jewelry, is the art of building metal forms, by electrodeposition, on a base or matrix. The matrix can be metal or an unorthodox material such as wood, paper, tinfoil, wax, or stryofoam. These materials can be left inside the newly electroformed piece, or they can be burned or melted out, leaving an extremely lightweight piece of jewelry.

This technique has unlimited possibilities for the invention of jewelry forms hitherto unachievable by traditional methods. Many soft materials, such as coal and porcelain, which break easily and have been nearly impossible to mount, can now be "set" by electroforming.

The pin above by Stanley Lechtzin was made over a matrix of stryofoam. The piece is white on white, formed of fine (pure) silver with an opalescent moonstone. It is extremely lightweight, and its interplay of texture and color is highly subtle and elegant. For this technique see pages 78–81.

combined methods

Many of the jewelry techniques are sufficient within themselves to produce pieces of character, strength, and beauty. Such techniques can also be combined to enrich a surface, add a color, accentuate or minimize a heavy positive shape with a linear form, or contrast a sleek area with a textured surface.

Materials such as wood, ivory, and gemstones combined with the standard metals further increase the craftsman's variety of selection.

Forging with granulation, silver inlaid with wood or ivory, cloisonné added to a cast pin, or a thin plane of ebony imbedded in a cast necklace are only a few of the many possibilities when combining methods and materials.

The pendant shown above, by John Paul Miller, is an example of three techniques skillfully combined—forging, granulation, and cloisonné. The wire cloisons, for the most part, do not touch which is a departure from the usual. See pages 82–85.

Photograph by Ferdinand Boesch

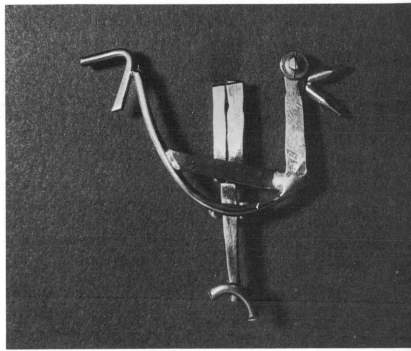

Photograph by Dave Kroening

lapidary

Lapidary refers to the art of cutting gem stones or to one who cuts, polishes, and engraves them.

Gem stones are of mineral origin and are graded as to color, luster, durability, and rarity into the categories, precious and semiprecious.

Traditionally, precious stones had been limited to four: ruby, sapphire, emerald, and diamond. Opal was sometimes included in this group but only when of a very superior quality, and, although a pearl is of organic origin, and therefore not a gem stone, it too, had been considered part of this group.

Today, the distinction between precious and semi-precious stones is very slight, and their division not very meaningful.

The pendant above, by Margaret De Patta, combines two stones, onyx and rutilated quartz, set in yellow gold. In this deceptively simple piece the stones seem to be liberated from their setting and to be floating in space. See pages 86–89.

found object jewelry

Found object jewelry is made from any material not orginally intended as jewelry. Museum examples of the work of early man abound in the ornaments he made out of the materials surrounding him—bone, ivory, wood, grasses, shells, and seeds.

Craftsmen today are showing new interest in using found objects and are artfully arranging them in contemporary settings. Nails, watch crystals, cloth, glass, and papier mâché are but a few of the additions to the natural materials used in the past.

Adapting common materials and converting them into jewelry can be a challenging experience, and jewelry so made can be informal or formal, whimsical or elegant.

The forged pin shown above, by Richard Schwanke, uses such found objects as galvanized wire and nails. The piece has all the quality of jewelry, and it is only after close examination that one becomes aware of the materials used. See pages 90–93.

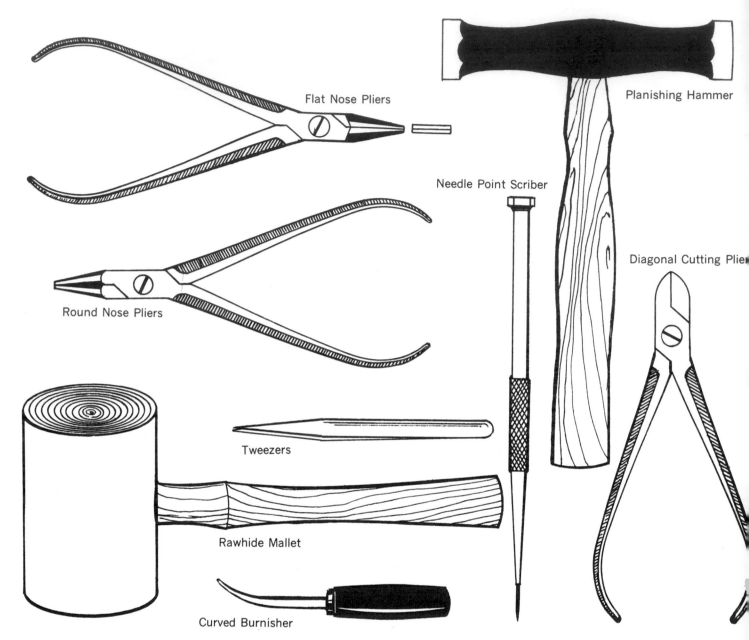

Flat Nose Pliers

Planishing Hammer

Needle Point Scriber

Round Nose Pliers

Diagonal Cutting Pliers

Tweezers

Rawhide Mallet

Curved Burnisher

tools and materials

The making of jewelry requires few tools; some of them are illustrated and listed here. Not all of the tools and materials listed throughout the book are essential; many of them serve special purposes and can be purchased when actually needed.

Flat Nose Pliers—with flat jaws, for shaping and bending metal.

Round Nose Pliers—with round jaws, for shaping metal to a curve.

Diagonal Cutting Pliers—for clipping and cutting wire.

Tweezers—two types, fine pointed and locking, for placing solder and picking up hot metal.

Rawhide Mallet—leather hammer to bend and hammer metal with a minimum of stretching and without leaving surface marks.

Curved Burnisher—for smoothing and polishing hard-to-get-at metal areas and mounting stones.

Needle Point Scriber—for positioning small pieces of solder and marking or drawing lines on metal.

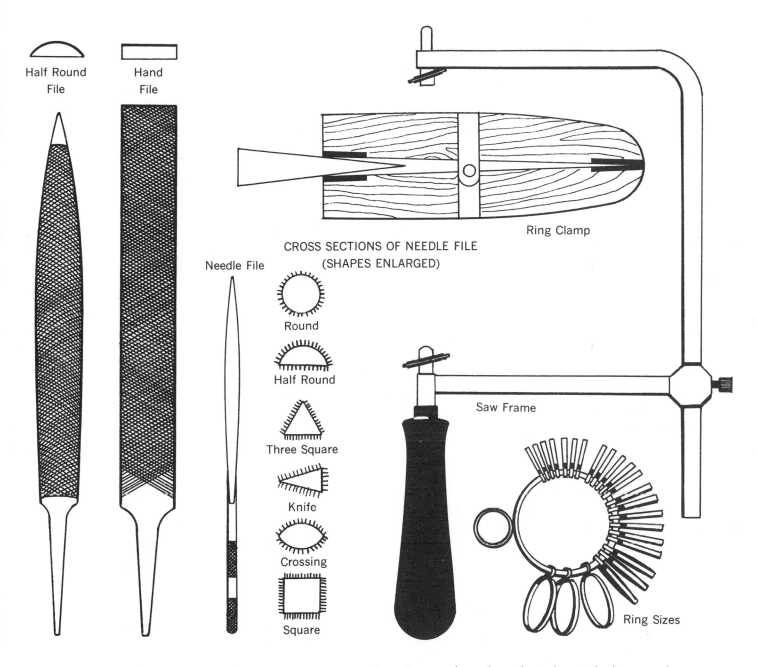

Half Round File

Hand File

Needle File

CROSS SECTIONS OF NEEDLE FILE
(SHAPES ENLARGED)

Round

Half Round

Three Square

Knife

Crossing

Square

Ring Clamp

Saw Frame

Ring Sizes

Planishing Hammer—for forging, has two faces to head, one flat, the other slightly belled.

Files—an assortment should include one 6″ hand file, one 6″ half round file, and a number of needle files. The latter can be purchased in almost any geometric cross sectional shape and are used for finishing small and delicate areas.

Ring Clamp—holds rings, pins, and other small pieces to be filed, sawed, or buffed.

Saw Frame and Blades—both come in various sizes, frame holds blades, and is adjustable.

Ring Sizes—series of graduated metal rings, each marked with a standard ring size.

Ring Mandrel—tapered steel rod marked with graduated ring sizes, for sizing, stretching, and shaping rings.

Bezel Mandrel—small tapered steel rod, used in making bezels, small rings, and for shaping.

Hand drill—all purpose, can be interchanged with numerous drills and burs.

Steel Rule—6″ length, is marked in millimeters and inches.

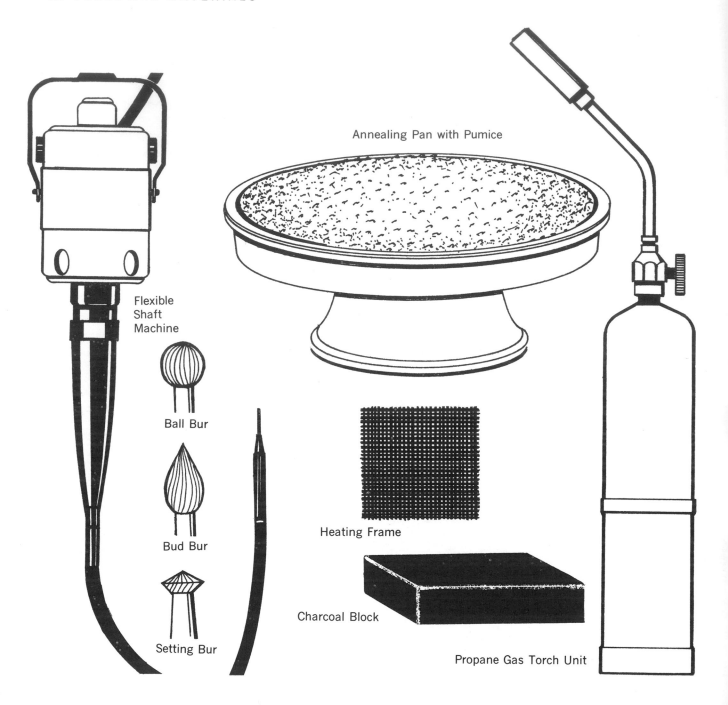

Flexible
Shaft
Machine

Ball Bur

Bud Bur

Setting Bur

Annealing Pan with Pumice

Heating Frame

Charcoal Block

Propane Gas Torch Unit

Flexible Shaft Machine—A Multipurpose Tool—eliminates hand operations such as drilling, grinding and buffing, is electrically operated, and includes a foot controlled rheostat to regulate the speed. A variety of files, drills, and burs are available.

Some of the tools used in this craft are used by your dentist as well, and you might check with him for files or for drills and burs needed for the flexible shaft machine. These tools, that the dentist must replace fairly frequently, have many hours of useful work in them for the jeweler.

MATERIALS:

Beeswax—a lubricant for saw blades. **White Casein**—used in transferring designs to metal. **Sable Brush (#6)** to apply casein. **Clear Acrylic Spray**—a fixative for transferred design. **Felt Buffing Stick**—for polishing by hand. **Emery Cloth, Paper, or Stick**—for removing scratches. The stick holds strips of emery cloth or paper, gives a flat surface on which to work. **Liver of Sulfur**—combines in a solution to oxidize metals. **Findings**—commercial fastenings such as cuff link backs, catches, pinstems, earring backs, and clasps.

SOLDERING TOOLS:

Heating Frame—a wire screen, used so that heat can reach under piece being soldered.

Charcoal Block—gives a good working surface, will not burn.

Annealing Pan—rotating pan, holds pumice. The rotation helps to distribute heat to piece being worked. Pumice can be shifted about to hold work in position.

Propane Gas Torch Unit—contains bottled gas, has adjustable flame tip.

MATERIALS:

Solder—a metal or metallic alloy which when melted joins metallic surfaces.

Flux—applied by sable brush to metal prior to heating.

Yellow Ochre—used to prevent solder from flowing in previously soldered areas.

Iron Binding Wire—holds pieces together for soldering.

safety

There are few hazards in the making of jewelry, but those few require precautions. These safety rules should be carefully read and followed.

NOTE: SPAREX, a non-corrosive, dry granulated powder, can be used instead of sulfuric acid for pickling. It does not contain acid and has the advantage of being noninflammable, nonexplosive and may be stored safely. It can be used over and over. Directions for mixing with water are on the container.

ACID

Acid is a dangerous substance and should be treated with respect. When an acid solution is to be made ALWAYS ADD ACID SLOWLY TO WATER, NEVER THE REVERSE. If done in reverse, acid may splash and even explode since acid and water combined generate heat.

When dropping metal into acid, use a glass jar with a lid. Place the jar at arm's length and hold the lid upended on the rim as a shield between you and the acid.

Keep acid solution covered with a lid to prevent the inhalation of fumes. Work near a window or fan in order to ventilate the area.

When heating acid solution in a pyrex container, use an electric hot plate, since the container is less likely to crack on this than on a gas burner.

Acid is extremely corrosive, so avoid contact with skin and clothing. Should acid get on your skin, flush immediately with running water and neutralize with bicarbonate of soda. Always keep bicarbonate of soda handy. Should acid enter your eye, put your head under a faucet and let the running water wash your eye. Should acid splash on your clothes, neutralize with bicarbonate of soda.

ELECTRICAL GRINDING

When grinding with an electrical tool, always wear plastic shatterproof goggles to protect your eyes from foreign matter.

SAWING AND FILING

Keep your fingers out of the direct path of saws and needle files.

SOLDERING

Follow the directions printed on the propane tank for proper handling. When lighting the torch, point the tip away from you. When you have finished using it, place it away from your immediate working area since the tip will still be hot.

Lid upended to shield against acid splashings.

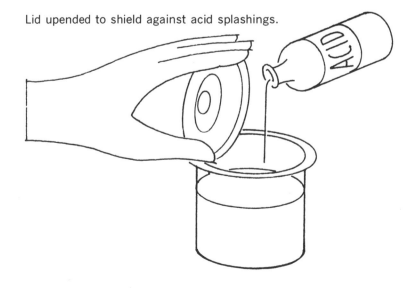

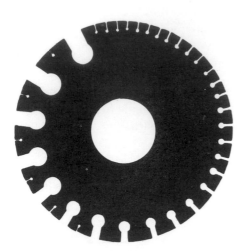

Browne and Sharpe gauge
for measuring the
thickness of metals

Browne and Sharpe gauge and shape chart

SHEET	
12	▬▬▬▬▬▬▬
14	▬▬▬▬▬▬▬
16	▬▬▬▬▬▬
18	▬▬▬▬▬
20	▬▬▬▬
22	▬▬▬
24	▬▬
26	▬

ROUND WIRE		SQUARE WIRE		HALF ROUND WIRE	
9	●	8	■	5/16″	◗
12	●	12	■	6	◗
16	•	14	▪	10	◗
18	•	18	▪	15	◗
20	•				
24	·				

metals

The techniques and methods described in this book deal with four metals: brass, copper, silver, and gold, but there are numerous other metals that can be used in the fabrication of jewelry such as platinum, stainless steel, niello, and iron.

Each metal has its own properties of color, hardness, and warmth and the appropriateness of these to the piece being made should be considered. Brass and copper, for example, will turn the finger green and should not be used for rings. Silver tarnishes, but whether it is made into a ring or a pin, continual wearing will keep its upper surface well polished. Pure gold is the most malleable and ductile of all metals and can be hammered into semi-transparent gold leaf but, like fine silver, it is too soft for most jewelry purposes. Therefore, for usability gold is alloyed. The alloys, copper, zinc, silver, and nickel, besides adding hardness to gold, bring a color change as well which results in red or rose gold, green gold, yellow gold, and white gold.

It is interesting that when brass and 14K yellow gold sheet metals are unpolished, it is difficult to tell the difference between them.

When a ring is finished its surface is smooth and polished, but in time scratches will appear and it will look as if the ring has to be rebuffed. Eventually, however, the entire surface will become slightly marked and will develop a soft luster which in a sense is a patina.

Platinum is an extremely hard metal; it does not scratch easily and can take a tremendous amount of abuse.

Stainless steel, a nonprecious metal, is also extremely hard, and requires special tools for easy handling. For that reason, and because it is a recently developed metal, it is being used by few craftsmen at present. It does have two distinct advantages, however; it does not scratch, and it can be formed with extreme thinness.

Niello, which is manufactured by the craftsman in his studio, is a steel grey-black metal and although it is too brittle to make complete pieces of jewelry from, it can be inlaid in intricate designs.

Iron, which is a comparatively crude metal, can be used with uncut stones to maintain a rough, vital quality. The black color of iron has been used quite successfully to offset diamonds. Since iron rusts, it requires some protection; but the rust may be considered as a patina.

Metals can be purchased in sheet or wire form. Sheet comes in various gauges or thicknesses and wires in round, square, half round and tubular shapes. Their thickness is measured by a wire and sheet gauge. Gauges vary by country; in the United States the Browne and Sharpe (B&S) wire gauge is the standard one used to measure silver, gold, copper, and their alloys. The gauge has measured slots of different widths on its circumference into which the wire or sheet is inserted.

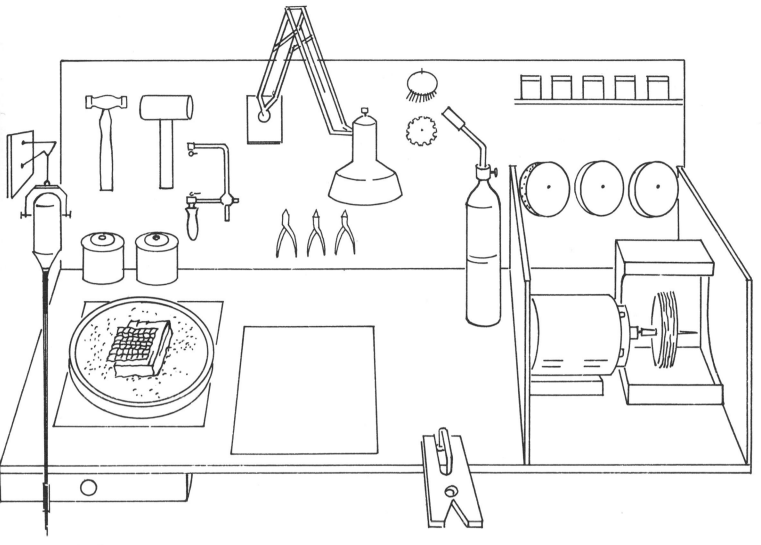

workshop

The drawing above is a suggestion for a compact and efficient workshop.

The work area should be near a window for light and ventilation. For additional light an adjustable lamp can be clamped to the bench or attached to the wall.

The workbench, of ¾″ plywood, can be secured to the wall as shown or put on legs of white pine 2x4″s. Clamped to it is a removable bench pin.

Tools hung conveniently on a peg board can be found quickly when needed. The buffing area is enclosed to shield the work area from flying dust and compounds.

The flexible shaft machine is hung from the wall for easy accessibility.

A portable workshop

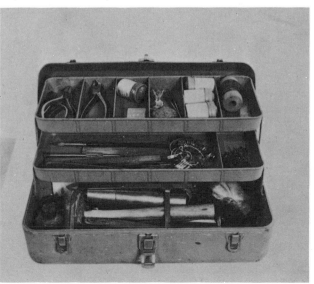

sawing

Sawing is a technique that can be mastered quickly, enabling you to saw precisely along any line or cut out any shape.

Tools: Saw frame, saw blades— #4/0 (fine) to #4 (coarse), hand drill or flexible shaft machine, ring clamp, and bench pin.
Materials: Beeswax

Inserting the Saw Blade

Inserting the saw blade properly is important. First loosen the wing screws at each end of the saw frame, then insert one end of the blade into the top of the frame, and tighten the top screw. The blade should be inserted with the teeth pointing outward from the frame and downward. If the direction of the teeth is difficult to determine, run your finger lightly over the surface of the blade. Brace the frame against the edge of the workbench and press it so that it is slightly compressed, then insert the other end of the blade. Tighten bottom wing screw and release pressure. The blade should be taut in the frame and, if at the proper tension, will make a pinging sound when plucked.

Sawing

You may find it easier to begin a cut with a few upward strokes of the blade, but the actual sawing is done on the downstroke. WHEN SAWING, HOLD THE SAW FRAME VERTICALLY. This helps to control the sawing and minimize blade breakage.

When a right angle is desired, or any extreme angle such as an obtuse, saw a straight line along one leg of the angle to the point of turning, then saw up and down in the same place without exerting forward pressure and slowly turn the saw in the new direction. Sawing curves should present no problems and you will develop your own technique of holding either the metal or the saw stationary while the other moves, or else move both at the same time.

Let the blade take its own cutting force; do not force it or exert forward pressure. Too much pressure will cause the blade to break.

There are two ways to remove the blade from a cut after sawing partially through a piece. Either move the saw blade up and down while backing out along the cut or loosen the wing screw, release the saw blade from one end of the frame, and pull the blade through.

Piercing

When a shape is to be cut from the center of the metal, the first step is to make a dent, with a center punch or nail, at a convenient point within the area to be cut out. Pierce a small hole through the dent with a hand drill or flexible shaft machine. The dent will prevent the drill from slipping over the surface of the metal. Release the saw blade from one end of the frame, insert it through the hole, and tighten back into position. Proceed with sawing in the usual manner and when it is completed, release the saw blade once more and remove the cut out metal, or negative shape.

Direction of pressure on saw frame during insertion of saw blade.

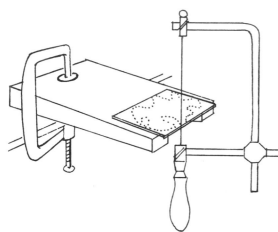

Sawing sheet metal using the workbench as a support.

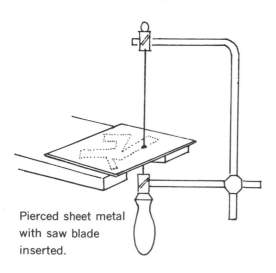

Pierced sheet metal with saw blade inserted.

Transferring Design to Metal

Once the design has been established, it is traced onto the metal or drawn freehand with a scriber. Complete directions are given on page 41, step 1.

Beeswax

Beeswax can be used occasionally to lubricate the blade. Knick the block of beeswax with the bottom third of the blade; take only a small amount as too much will clog the saw teeth. The sawing action of the blade will melt the wax and carry it along the entire sawing surface. Beeswax is not necessary when sawing thin gauge metals, but sawing #6 gauge or heavier will be made considerably easier.

Bench Pin

The bench pin supports the metal being sawed. It is a small, wooden wedge with a V-shaped opening and is fastened with a C clamp to the workbench. Bench pins can be bought inexpensively or cut from white pine.

Ring Clamp

The ring clamp acts as an extension of the hand and is indispensible for holding small work. It is usually made from a hard wood such as maple, and its jaws have leather insets to prevent the metal from being scratched. One end is rounded, the other squared, and a wedge can be inserted into either one leaving the other free to grip the work.

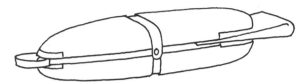

Ring clamp holding work in position.

filing

Forms are shaped by files, curves are cut, contours rounded, edges beveled, and planes smoothed. Files are also used after sawing to refine forms or to correct them where necessary. They come in various shapes, sizes, and cutting grades. In general when you have a good deal of filing to do, begin with a coarse file, and then use finer grades to finish up the surface.

Tools: 6″ hand file, needle files, half round file, vise, and ring clamp.

Hold the work in your hand, in a vise, or in a ring clamp. The last two are effective for pieces too small to be hand-held. A bench pin or the edge of the workbench can be used to support the metal.

Files are designed to work away from you on the forward stroke only. Start at the tip of the file and work toward the handle, exerting firm pressure in that direction. At the end of the stroke, you can either lift the file from the work, or you can reduce pressure and slide the file toward you, then resume pressure on the forward stroke.

In order to make the surfaces of a piece parallel, file them across a 6″ hand file placed on the workbench, this is especially appropriate when filing a ring.

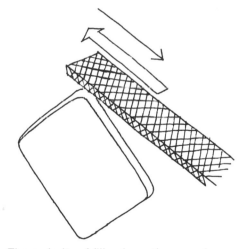

The majority of filing is on the away-from-you stroke.

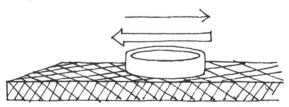

Filing the edge of a ring flush against a 6″ hand file.

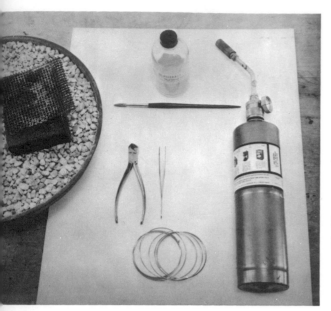

Soldering equipment: Bottle of flux, sable brush, tweezers, clipping pliers, torch, wire solder, heating frame over charcoal block in pumice pan.

Sheet solder inscribed with S, M, and H to keep the soft, medium and hard solders from becoming mixed.

soldering

Soldering is the method used to unite metal surfaces by heat and solder. There are many different types of solder, but this book will deal with the three basic ones—soft, medium, hard—or #1, #2, #3. These grades represent different melting temperatures and are used successively when a piece is soldered more than once.

For example, when soldering a piece of work requiring three solder joints, you would use hard solder for the first joint since it has the highest melting point, medium solder for the second joint since it requires less heat, and soft solder for the third joint.

If heat is applied carefully, however, several solder joints in the same piece can be worked with the same grade solder.

Tools: Propane soldering torch, charcoal block, heating frame, pumice pan, tweezers.
Materials: Flux with sable brush, solder, iron binding wire—26 gauge, emery cloth—fine, ammonia.

When working with silver or gold, use silver or gold solder to insure that the color at the joint will be consistent with the color of the metal. Silver solder can also be used with brass and copper but, for the times when the differences in color will not be desirable, solders closer to the metal colors can be obtained.

Solders come in stick, wire, or sheet form. Since these solders melt at different temperatures they should be kept in separate containers, but for sheet solder just scratch the letters S, M, or H on them.

If the solder has been cut into small pieces and you think the grades may have been mixed, it is better to discard them rather than take the chance of having a missolder.

Melting temperature of silver solder:

Soft (#1)	1325° F
Medium (#2)	1390° F
Hard (#3)	1425° F

There are five important steps to remember when soldering:
1. **Fitting**—Fit tightly together all surfaces to be soldered.
2. **Cleaning**—Remove all surface dirt and grease.
3. **Fluxing**—Apply flux to metal and solder.
4. **Solder Positioning**—Place solder in the correct positions and amounts.
5. **Heating**—Use torch to heat the metal quickly to a temperature in which solder will melt and flow.

Fitting

It is imperative that all surfaces to be soldered together fit closely along their whole length and width. Occasionally as in a ring, ends may have to be held together with iron binding wire. There can be no gaps, and any irregularities will have to be removed by filing. Where necessary, the binding wire is also used to hold pieces in position while being soldered. Solder will not adhere to iron binding wire. It comes in various gauges, but for general use #26 gauge is sufficient.

Cleaning

Surfaces that are to be soldered together must be perfectly clean. All traces of grease, dirt, or fingerprints must be removed in order for the solder to flow properly. The surfaces can be cleaned with a soft-bristled toothbrush dipped in ammonia solution (regular household ammonia diluted with water) and then rinsed well in running water. Another method is to place the metal in acid for a few minutes, or sand the surfaces with emery cloth. These methods can be followed by placing the piece directly on a charcoal block, or on a heating frame which is then placed on a charcoal block, and brushing it lightly with the torch flame to burn off any remaining grease. This takes only a few seconds and must not be done for longer or fire scale could form.

Fluxing

Flux, a glasslike material that comes in paste or liquid form, is applied to all metal and solder surfaces to prevent fire scale and to help the solder flow. To facilitate covering surfaces, hold the pieces with tweezers. Apply flux with a sable brush used only for this purpose.

If the piece is not well covered, more flux can be added during the first heating stages. Brush on the addition quickly and lightly, otherwise the brush will burn and leave a residue on the metal. A liquid flux, such as hard solder flux, combines several fluxing properties and not only helps keep fire scale from forming, but chemically cleans the surfaces by absorbing fire scale as the metal is heated.

Heating

The piece ready for heating can be placed on a pumice pan (a rotating annealing pan filled with pumice), on an asbestos block, or on a charcoal block, with or without a heating frame. Or place the heating frame directly on the pumice pan and scoop out the pumice under the frame so that the torch can be directed beneath it when necessary.

Bathe the piece in flame using a rotating motion of the torch. The medium tip of the Bernz-O-Matic torch is good for this work. When solder is almost ready to flow, bring the torch in closer and concentrate it on the flow area. If this is not done, the heat will dissipate into the entire piece and it will take the metal longer to reach the flow temperature of solder. This temperature should be reached quickly or the flux will "wear out" and its action will be lost.

The melting temperature of solder can be determined by the color of the metal which is seen best in subdued light. Metal, as it is being heated, ranges in color from a deep dull red at its coolest to a bright cherry red which indicates that solder should be flowing. Beyond, there is the risk that metal will turn white and reach its melting point.

If solder has not flowed by the time the metal turns bright cherry red, something was not done properly—either in fluxing or cleaning, or the heating was not done quickly enough and the solder deteriorated.

SOLDER POSITIONS and direction of heat for three conditions. The entire piece is heated and the flame directed as shown. Solder always flows toward the source of heat.

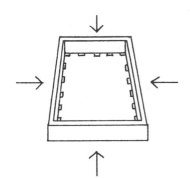

1. Solder placement for bezel.

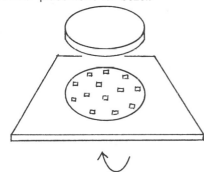

2. Solder placement for flat surface.

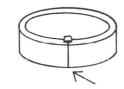

3. Solder placement for ring joint.

Typical flame from propane torch.

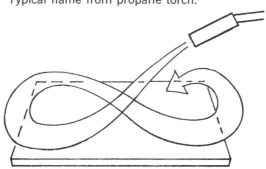

Rotation of flame for heating piece of work.

Another way to determine when metal is reaching a temperature for solder to begin to flow is by the flux which will turn white from the heat and then become transparent and glasslike.

Solder is flowing properly when you see either the metal piece drop into position or a bright silver line along the solder seam.

Sweat Soldering

Sweat soldering is generally applied to broad flat surfaces which are to be joined together.

Position solder for sweat soldering. As in all soldering a complete bond is desired. If the work has points or extensions of metal, place a piece of solder as far towards the end of it as possible. Flux work as well as solder. Place solder on back side of upper plate.

Heat the work using a circular or rotating motion to distribute heat evenly. Apply heat until solder just begins to flow, then immediately remove heat, leaving small mounds of solder.

Clean work in acid solution, neutralize, and wipe dry. Run solder mounds over the surface of a 6″ hand file to remove excess solder and to flatten mounds slightly. Be sure not to remove too much solder or not enough will remain to bind the work together.

The work is fluxed, placed together, heated, and the solder permitted to flow. After soldering, the work will be joined, leaving a fine solder seam. Once the piece is buffed the seam will be nearly invisible. The lower plate can be left somewhat larger than the upper plate and filed after the work is joined, to ensure exact fit.

Pickling

Between solderings, the work is pickled in acid solution to remove oxides (fire scale) and used fluxes. Mix the solution in a pyrex container.

Pickling solution: 10 parts cold water
1 part sulfuric acid

CAUTION—ADD ACID SLOWLY TO THE WATER, NEVER THE REVERSE. If done in reverse, acid can splash or even explode due to chemical reaction. See safety precautions, page 19.

SPAREX, a non-corrosive and very effective pickling solution can be substituted for sulfuric acid. It comes in granulated form and dilutes in water. It is also excellent for use in the classroom.

The work can be dropped into the pickle while still hot from soldering but after losing its cherry red color. You can also drop the work into the pickle cold, then heat the solution. Use a hot plate since pyrex containing acid is less likely to crack on this than on a gas burner.

The container should have a lid to prevent the inhalation of fumes and evaporation of the solution. Also use the lid as a shield when dropping hot metal into the pickling solution.

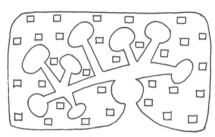

Solder placed on back of upper plate

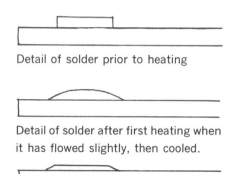

Detail of solder prior to heating

Detail of solder after first heating when it has flowed slightly, then cooled.

Detail of mound flattened after filing

After pickling is completed, remove the work and neutralize it in a solution of 2 cups water to 2 heaping tbsp. sodium bicarbonate. If the sodium bicarbonate (baking soda) is added to warm water, it will dissolve more easily.

Use copper, nickel, or brass tongs or tools to remove work from the pickle. Never allow steel or iron to come in contact with the pickle for a chemical reaction results producing copper stains on the work.

Findings

Most jewelry require fastenings to hold them in place: backs for cuff links, clasps for earrings, stems and catches for pins. There are numerous other fastenings, also called findings, on the market. Available in silver or gold, even the best quality is not too expensive.

In some cases when the finding remains visible or forms an integral part of the design, you may prefer to make your own.

Since findings are fragile and melt easily, they are generally soldered in place with #1 solder. For some findings soldering is sufficient, but others require both soldering and riveting. For example, the spring device on a cuff link back will lose its tension if heated; therefore, first the joint is soldered in place, then the back is inserted in the joint and two riveted together. When using a catch, joint, and pinstem, the catch and joint are soldered in place, and the pinstem is riveted into the joint since the pinstem will also lose its tension if heated. For riveting pinstem, see page 32.

Soldering Findings: Two Methods

1. Flux the piece and heat it until the flux turns white. Cut pieces of solder slightly larger than the base of each finding and flux. They are then placed in position at opposite ends on the back of the work with a pair of tweezers. Since the flux on the piece will be dry, the wet flux on the solder will cause the solder to adhere in position.

Heat the piece allowing the solder to flow slightly, as in directions for sweat soldering. This includes the filing away of excess solder. Pickle the piece and reflux. Place the findings on top of the solder, keeping the catch closed to prevent the solder from flowing into the mechanism and freezing it. Heat the piece until the solder flows. The findings at this point may slip slightly out of position and can be realigned with the tip of a scribe. Heat the tip first for if it is cool it will absorb the heat from the findings and cool them so that they chill or freeze the solder.

2. A more direct method, but somewhat more difficult, is to place the findings directly on the molten solder. The fluxed solder is first put on the fluxed piece and heated until it flows. The findings in this case, would be soldered on, one at a time, each finding heated simultaneously with the piece.

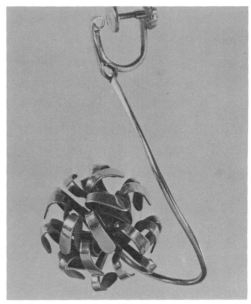

Forged silver earring by Merry Renk. Note how the commercial finding works as an integral part of the design.

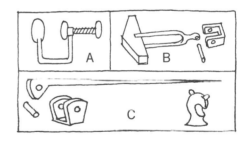

A. Screw type earring back.
B. Cuff link back, rivet and joint.
C. Pinstem, rivet, joint, and catch.

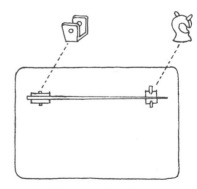

Placement of joint and catch onto the upper third of the back of pin.

Forged gold brooch, by Naomi Davis. Note how high buff finish enhances the work. Photograph by Murray Weiss.

buffing

Applying the final finish to the piece is the last basic step in jewelry making. First all scratch marks, excess solder, and surface blemishes are removed with fine files and emery cloth.

Tools: Buffing motor, buffing wheels, files.
Materials: Buffing compounds, emery cloth, soft bristle brush, ammonia.

Buffing Compounds

The compounds range in grade from the very coarse to the very fine; three of them are listed here:

1. **Tripoli**—removes emery cloth scratches and leaves an unblemished finish.
2. **Red Rouge**—polishes to a high finish.
3. **White Rouge**—polishes to a brilliant mirrorlike finish.

It is not necessary to use all the polishing compounds to obtain the final finish, but the ones used are applied in the above order. You do not, for example, skip tripoli and go directly to red rouge. White rouge has a brilliant finish that tends to destroy the soft luster of metal, but there may be times when you will find this finish desirable.

The abrasive action of buffing compounds can create small streaks or feathering in the metal. Constantly rotating the piece during buffing should prevent this; this is particularly important when removing small pits or scratches from the metal.

Machine Buffing

Buffing can be done with an electric motor purchased new or secondhand. A secondhand motor is inexpensive and, with the addition of a tapered spindle to hold the buffing wheels, converts easily to a buffing machine. The direction of wheel rotation should be towards you, from the top down. A good speed to maintain is about 1725 rpm; do not exceed 3450 rpm as metal wears away too quickly at this speed.

Buffing motor with buffing wheel and hood. Shaded area on wheel indicates buffing area.

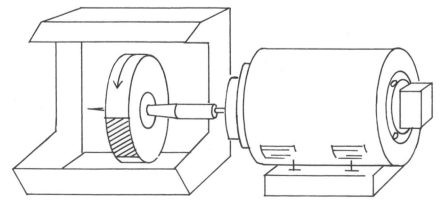

Breaking in a Buffing Wheel

Turn on the motor. Place a buffing wheel on the spindle and apply a compound to it in moderation. During this operation an excess of lint will fly off the wheel and loose fibers will protrude.

Turn off the motor. Burn the loose fibers with a match. Do this in small sections at a time and extinguish the flame quickly as you go, tapping with your hand. Be careful not to turn on the motor during the burning process for the flames will quickly burn holes in the buff.

Repeat this operation until no loose fibers protrude from the wheel. It is advisable to test the wheel on spare metal to see if it is polishing smoothly.

Applying Compounds

The compounds are applied to the wheels during buffing as needed. Apply only in moderate amounts; too much will cake the wheels.

Wheels and compounds should not be interchanged; each compound has its own wheel. Wash work free of various compounds and rouges during changing wheels and after final polishing. This can be done with a fine-bristled nylon toothbrush which has been dipped into a solution of household ammonia and water. If the work becomes too hot during buffing, dip it in water to cool.

Holding the Work

Hold the work securely in your hands, or in a ring clamp if it is too small to be hand-held. Do not buff into edges as this will wear away sharp detail and form. As a safety precaution always position the work toward the bottom of the wheel so that if it is pulled from your hands, it will be thrown onto the working surface and not towards you. Shatterproof plastic goggles will protect your eyes from flying compounds and dust.

The correct way to secure a chain for polishing is to wrap it firmly around a board with the loose ends held tightly in your hands. If necessary, polish the chain a section at a time.

Holding the chain in this manner will prevent accidents. Keep in mind that the wheel is rotating at a minimum of 1725 rpm, and if the lengths are torn from your hands they can harm you and possibly foul up the motor.

Hand Buffing

Polishing by hand can be done with a felt buffing stick to which tripoli has been applied and then with a rouge-impregnated felt cloth. Although hand buffing leaves a fine finish on the metal, a motor is quicker and more efficient to use.

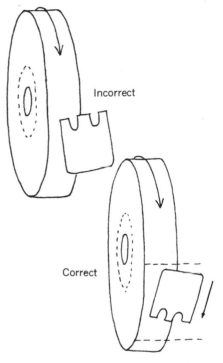

Incorrect

Correct

Sawed or filed areas should be held in the direction of the wheel's rotation.

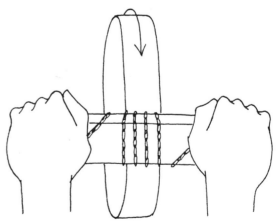

To secure a chain for buffing, hold ends tightly in your hands.

oxidizing

Oxidizing refers to coloring metals with chemicals to create contrasts and should be considered when working with silver forms that are too small or their designs too complicated for tarnish to be removed easily. Tarnishing is a slow form of oxidation.

Coloring the metals takes place only after all the basic work has been completed. The work to be treated must be absolutely clean and free of any oil or grease. This is best assured by scrubbing with a toothbrush dipped in ammonia and water, then rinsing off the solution.

Tools: Tweezers, sable brush
Materials: Liver of sulfur (potassium sulfide), ammonia, emery cloth

Making the Solution

The most popular oxidizing material used to darken silver and the one easiest to prepare is potassium sulfide, commonly called liver of sulfur. Its color range is from bluish grey to black. Liver of sulfur is obtainable in crystal form and dilutes in water to any strength desired. However a solution that is extremely strong could cause flaking.

Directions for mixing strengths are generally given on the label; if not, test solutions can be made.

Liver of sulfur in its diluted and undiluted form should be kept in dark air-tight bottles, away from light, to prevent deterioration.

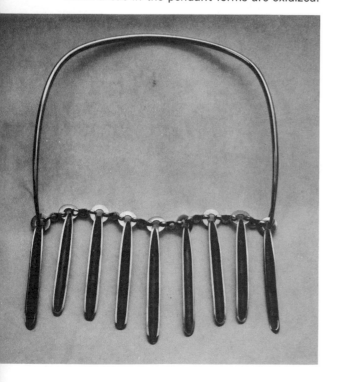

Stainless steel necklace, by Mary Ann Scherr. Black areas in the pendant forms are oxidized.

Coloring the Metal

Once the solution is diluted, apply with a brush to the areas which are to be darkened. If most of the surface is to be covered, it is quicker to place the entire piece into the solution and remove occasionally to check its progress. Use tweezers or a piece of silver wire for this and rinse them afterwards.

When oxidation is complete allow the piece to dry, then buff off oxidation in the areas where it is not wanted.

To speed up the oxidation process, the piece can be slightly heated with the tip of the torch before the liver of sulfur is brushed on or it can be dropped into a heated solution of liver of sulfur.

If too much heat is applied, the oxidation can flake or cover unevenly. In that case the piece would have to be buffed again and reoxidized. If the oxidation is extremely poor, the piece can be pickled, which will, of course, require it to be repolished. Try to avoid this, as excess buffing can wear away the crispness of your work.

bezels

The collar bezel is one of the earliest forms of bezels and the simplest to make for holding stones securely in place.

Bezel wire, made of fine or pure silver or pure gold and, therefore quite malleable, can be used for the collar bezels. Malleability is desirable since too great a pressure during the pressing inward of the bezel can cause the stone to crack.

Making a Collar Bezel

Determine the length of the bezel by wrapping a narrow strip of paper or metal around the circumference of the stone and marking it at the overlap. The bezel should be just deep enough to hold the stone securely, too deep a bezel will hide the stone and the bezel can easily wrinkle while being pushed into place.

Cut the bezel wire and file its ends perfectly parallel. It is then bent into a flattened oval so that its ends meet tightly thus insuring a good solder joint. Solder with hard solder. See soldering page 24. After the bezel has been pickled and rinsed, it is formed to fit the shape of the stone. This is done by putting it on a bezel mandrel. Mandrels are available in round, oval, and square shapes.

To make a square bezel mounting for a square stone, the corners of the bezel are partially filed out and nicked to allow the metal to be bent to form right angles.

The stone should be placed in the bezel to check its fit which should be snug without being forced. If the bezel is too small it can be stretched slightly by placing it on the mandrel and hammering it with a flat face of a planishing hammer. If it is too large, a piece of metal must be cut out, including the solder seam, and the joint resoldered.

When a bezel is to be soldered to a flat surface its base must be absolutely flat. In order to insure this, rub the base over emery cloth. If, however, it is to be soldered onto the ring shank (body of the ring), its base must be filed to the same curve as the ring.

When the bezel has been soldered into position, insert the stone and push it into place with a burnisher. The pressure of the burnisher while pushing the bezel inward around the stone must be even and sure since a slip could cause a soft stone to crack. Pushing in the bezel should begin at opposite points to keep the stone centered. Repeating this method in other areas will also prevent the bezel from wrinkling when smooth strokes are applied during the final pushing down of the bezel. As the burnisher is pushing the bezel in place, it is also polishing the metal. All the while the work should be firmly supported against the workbench. If the top edge of the bezel is uneven, smooth by running the tip of the burnisher around its rim.

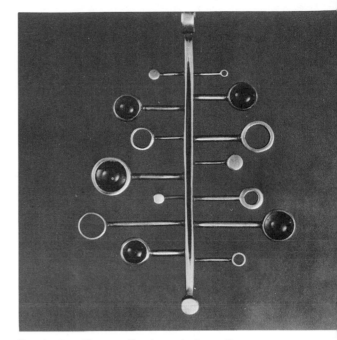

Pendant with amethysts set in collar bezels, by Frances Boothly. Photograph by Bob Hagerman.

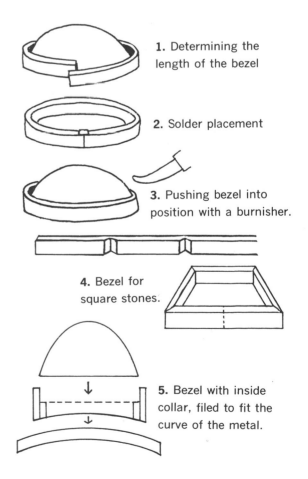

1. Determining the length of the bezel

2. Solder placement

3. Pushing bezel into position with a burnisher.

4. Bezel for square stones.

5. Bezel with inside collar, filed to fit the curve of the metal.

additional information

Drawplate

Although wire is available in many shapes and in a wide range of gauges, it is not always convenient to stock them all, particularly, if they are not used too often. With a drawplate, however, it becomes a simple matter to draw a heavier gauge wire to any smaller size.

A drawplate is a plate of hardened steel which has a series of holes, graduated in size, and tapered, from the back of the plate to the front. The holes may be round, half round, square, rectangular, or triangular. It is also possible to obtain drawplates that have several shapes on the same plate.

The wire is drawn through the holes of the drawplate with the aid of drawtongs which are heavy duty blunt nose pliers with a curved handle for better gripping and serrated jaws for holding the wire securely.

Beeswax is used to make drawing easier and to lengthen the life of the drawplate. Either rub it into the holes of the plate that the wire will pass through or pull the wire across a beeswax block.

The drawplate should be placed horizontally in a smooth-jawed vise, the smaller tapered end of the hole toward you. The vise should be clamped to a heavy bench, since pulling the wire can be strenuous enough to move a lighter bench.

File, or hammer, one inch at the end of the wire to an elongated point. This is done so that when the wire is inserted into the hole enough will protrude to be gripped by the tongs. Use just the amount of wire that can be drawn through in one steady pull.

Find the smallest hole that the wire will go through, then through the next smallest hole insert the pointed end of the wire from the back of the plate to the front. Grasp the protruding end with the drawtongs, and draw the wire through in one stroke while keeping it perpendicular to the drawplate. If the wire is not pulled through in one stroke, there will be a kink in it where the pull was interrupted. Put the wire through the next hole, do not skip a hole while reducing wire as this could cause the wire to break as well as damage the drawplate.

Continue this process until the wire has been reduced to the desired thickness. If it is to be reduced a good deal, it becomes brittle. Annealing will keep it soft and minimize the possibility of its breaking.

Rivets

Some pinstems are available with rivets already fixed in place. In that case it is a matter of squeezing the ends of the rivet flat with pliers so that they will stay permanently in position. Rivet-setting pliers may be used for this. Keep in mind that the pinstem is put in place after the catch and joint have been soldered to the work.

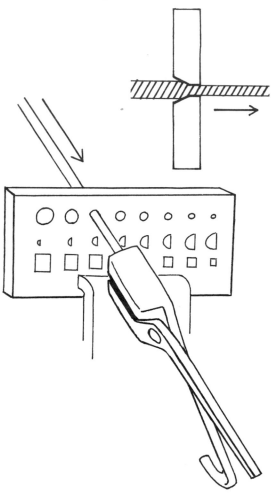

Cross section of drawplate with wire being drawn.

Drawplate showing various shapes with gradations and wire being drawn with drawtongs.

For pinstems that do not come so supplied, rivets are made by cutting a length of rivet wire or round wire of the same gauge as the hole in the joint. Place the pinstem between the soldered joint so that the holes in the stem and in the joint are aligned. In order that the rivet can move freely in the pinstem without breaking, the pinstem hole should be slightly larger than the holes in the joint.

Insert the wire through the holes to measure the correct length which should be 1/16″ beyond each end of the joint. The wire is then removed and clipped or sawed to the proper length.

With the pinstem still in position between the holes in the joint, reinsert the wire so that it extends the 1/16″ beyond each end. The work is now placed sideways on a steel block with one end of the protruding wire resting on the block. Tap the opposite end of the wire halfway down with the flat face of a planishing hammer. The pressure of the tapping will also compress the wire resting on the block.

Reverse the piece and continue hammering until the ends of the wire are spread flat over the holes to form a rivet.

Shortening the Pinstem

To shorten the pinstem to the proper length—it should not extend more than 1/32″ beyond the catch—clip off its end and file to a new point with a needle file. Rub with emery cloth until all file marks are removed and the point is smooth and sharp enough to penetrate a piece of fabric without damaging it.

Yellow Ochre

When soldering is to take place near a previously soldered joint, that joint can be kept from flowing by coating it with yellow ochre. The use of yellow ochre should be limited to the times when heat being applied in the area could cause solder to reflow or when the new joint and the previously soldered one use the same solder.

Yellow ochre comes in powdered form and is mixed with a small amount of water to a paste about the consistency of heavy cream. Apply with a brush onto the joint that is to be protected, but be sure that the ochre does not mix with the flux on the new joint as it will prevent the new solder from flowing.

The work must be heated slowly otherwise the ochre will pop off. Additional care must be taken during soldering as too much heat can cause the solder joints under the yellow ochre to collapse.

The ochre turns black from the heat as it burns on. If it does not come off during the pickling, scrub with a toothbrush.

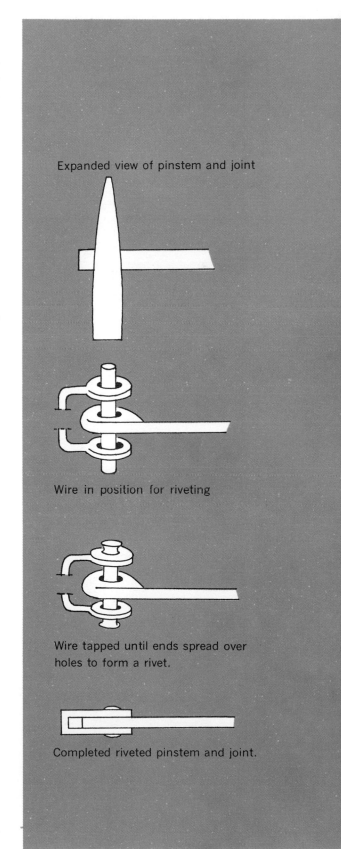

Expanded view of pinstem and joint

Wire in position for riveting

Wire tapped until ends spread over holes to form a rivet.

Completed riveted pinstem and joint.

Cuts made by engraving tools

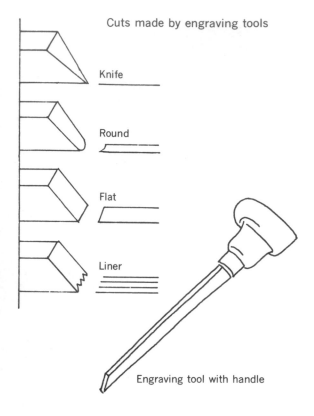

Knife

Round

Flat

Liner

Engraving tool with handle

Silver brooch, fish form with engraved design, Haida, British Columbia, Canada. Courtesy of The Museum of the American Indian, Heye Foundation.

surface treatments

Jewelry shaped by the basic processes make handsome finished pieces, but there are times when the craftsman will design a piece that includes treating the surface of the metal. The decision to use surface treatments should be planned as part of the initial design so that the body of the metal and the surface relate to each other.

Engraving

Engraving is a technique which cuts or incises lines into the surface of metal. Although the process is a simple one, such a considerable amount of practice is necessary in order to engrave successfully that it has become a highly specialized field of jewelry. However, with some study, it is possible to learn to engrave simply but well.

The tools used are called gravers. They are basically chisels set in wooden handles, each designed to produce a specific cut in the metal; to incise a design, texture a surface, and cut.

Both tools and handles are made in a variety of shapes, are purchased separately, and are fitted together by hammering the tool into a drilled hole in the handle. The graver is sharpened to the correct cutting angle before and during engraving by rubbing it on oilstone. The cutting angle should be no more than 45° in order to prevent the point of the tool from breaking.

A design can be drawn freehand on the metal with a scriber or transferred through white casein. See Transferring Design page 23. The metal is heated lightly with a torch, and while still warm, placed into a block of pitch which holds it in place while it is being engraved. The work may also be held in a shellac stick or in a ring clamp.

During engraving, hold the tool with the handle resting in the palm of your hand, the thumb laid partly on a side of the tool and partly on the block to control the cutting angle. Hold your other hand securely around the block, the tip of its thumb against the first thumb to steady it and to keep the tool from slipping.

To begin engraving, place the tool almost vertically to the work, lower it carefully to the correct cutting angle, and as the downward pressure increases, inch the tool forward into the metal.

Whether to turn the metal and the tool or to keep the tool stationary while the metal moves under it, is a matter of personal preference. The point is to maintain control over the tool.

Etching

Etching, a technique which produces a relief design to the surface of the metal by means of acid and an acid resist, is easier to master than engraving, but certainly no less effective. All metals can be etched, but silver, brass, and copper are simpler to use since they require less strong acids.

The metal is first cleaned thoroughly. Then, with a small sable brush, paint an acid resist of asphaltum on all areas that are to remain raised. This includes the back as well as the edges of the metal.

Acid solution formula for silver, brass, and copper metals:
1 part nitric acid
2 parts water
See safety precautions for acid, page 19.

Place the metal carefully in the acid solution. Almost immediately the unpainted areas will be attacked by the acid causing tiny bubbles to appear on the surface of the metal.

The strength of the solution and the length of time the piece is left in the acid will determine the depth of the etch. Check at intervals by lifting the piece from the acid with copper pickling tongs.

After the etch has eaten to the desired depth to produce the lowered areas of the design, remove the work and neutralize it in a solution of 1 tbs. sodium bicarbonate (baking soda) to 1 cup of water, then rinse in running water. The asphaltum can be removed with turpentine either by soaking the piece or rubbing it with a cloth.

Repoussé and Chasing

Repoussé is a method of working on the back of metal to produce a relief design to the surface. Chasing is worked on the face of the metal to texture it and sharpen the repoussé design. Both use punches that come in a variety of shapes and sizes and that work the metal while it is supported on pitch.

The pitch is heated lightly so that it does not burn—a pitch bowl may be used. Heat the metal after first tracing a design on it and press it firmly, design side up, on the pitch surface so that no spaces remain beneath. To assure even contact, raise some pitch over the edges of the metal. The pitch bowl can be held in a leather ring base which will permit it to be tilted at any angle.

The tool is set vertically to the work and slanted slightly. Tap it repeatedly with a small hammer, preferably a chasing hammer, while moving it over the design. As soon as the metal resists the punch it should be pried loose from the pitch and annealed. The pitch can be wiped off the metal with a turpentine-soaked cloth.

After annealing, replace the work in the pitch and continue punching out the design until the desired depth is reached. Remove, anneal, and then reverse the metal onto the pitch. The pitch may have to be heated until soft and then poured into the hollow areas of the metal in order to give them support. Work this side and refine the design with chasing tools. Hold the tools straight up and do not lift them from the metal. They are hammered slightly as they move in a continuous line.

When completed the piece is removed from the pitch, pickled, and then buffed.

Pin, of white gold with etched design by Thomas Gentille. Photograph by Ferdinand Boesch.

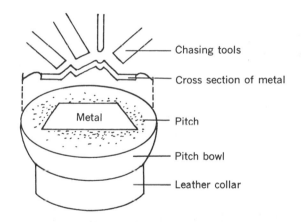

Chasing tools
Cross section of metal
Metal
Pitch
Pitch bowl
Leather collar

Gold plaque, repoussé, Panama. Courtesy of The Cleveland Museum of Art.

design

The jewelry pieces on the following four pages have a basic similarity—they are each based on an individual approach to design—stones that pivot, reflections for greater brilliance, degree of polishing, repeat of design, duality of purpose—these approaches become the starting points for the pieces and dictate the essential character of their forms.

Sculptural Form

The cast sterling silver pin by Jose de Rivera is a sculptural form and so graceful that it seems to be in flight. The illusion of motion is heightened by the high polishing of its sleek surfaces.

Geometric Forms

On the opposite page, in the necklace by Günther Wyss, a series of geometric forms repeat themselves and link together. The manner of linking produces interest and avoids a feeling of monotony. Again, as in the de Rivera pin, the construction of a piece is accentuated by its highly polished surfaces resulting in jewelry that is simple, sleek, and elegant. The structural piece by Günther Wyss also uses a series of geometric forms. It is a design unit of versatility and can be worn as a bracelet or displayed as an ornament. The fineness of its craftsmanship and its high finish accent its strong character.

Reflected Form

(Opposite) In the ring by Friedrich Becker, a pyramid-shaped 1.5 carat diamond is set so that its brilliance is reflected in a similar shape of white gold. The reflection of the diamond in the mirror finish of the gold's metal gives to the single stone a dazzling array of light play.

Repeat Motif

The nose ornament from Colombia (Calima) ca. 200 B.C. is made of gold beaten very thin and is, therefore, light in weight. In this piece one shape is repeated three times; it appears twice in the small upper areas and forms the entire shape of the main area. All the circular shapes and the pendant tubular ones are attached by gold wire and swing freely with every movement. (See page 38).

Variation of a Repeat Motif

The shoulder sash, Koasati, American Indian, 1825–1850, is a strip of wool decorated with red and white beads. This is a fine example of a repeat in design that is almost similar but because of a slight variation is never the same. (See page 38).

Cast pin by Jose de Rivera. Courtesy of Craft Horizons. Photograph by Ferdinand Boesch.

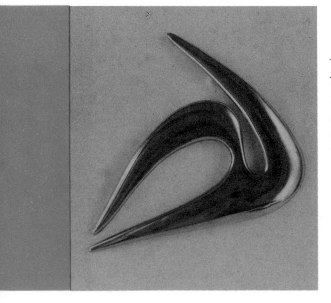

Ring by Friedrich Becker

Bracelet by Günther Wyss. Courtesy of Craft Horizons.

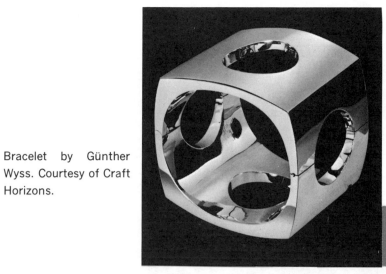

Necklace by Günther Wyss

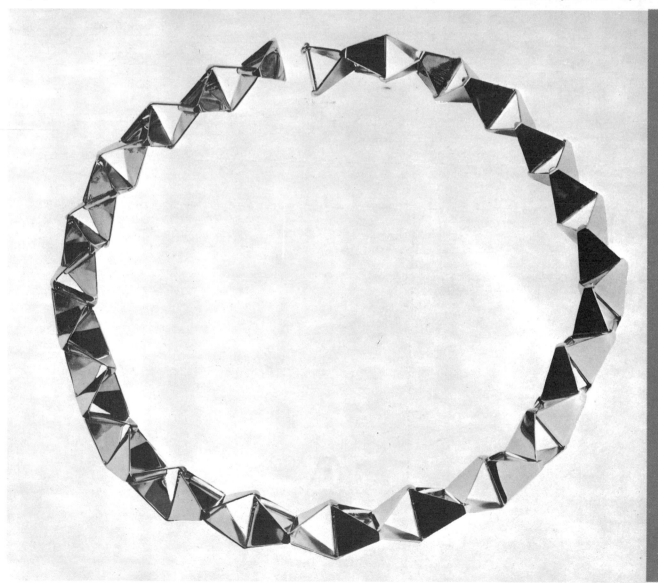

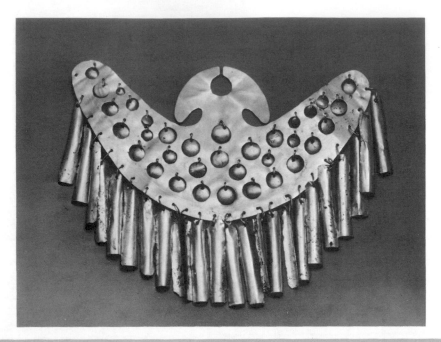

Nose ornament, Colombia (Calima) ca. 200 B.C. Courtesy of the Museum of Primitive Art.

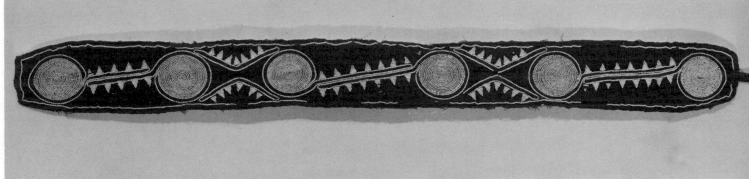

Shoulder sash, Koasati, American Indian, 1825–1850. Courtesy of the Museum of the American Indian. Heye Foundation

Gold pendant, Panama. Courtesy of the Museum of Primitive Art.

Symmetrical Form

The gold pendant from Panama, is a symmetrical design in the shape of two 'birds and is an example of abstracting an idea from nature. It has fine detailing and a feeling of great strength. The piece is barely polished and if it had received a high polish much of its beauty would have been lost.

Dual Purpose Design

The earrings of Irene Brynner are gold with amethyst and pearls. They are slipped over the earlobe where they are held in place by a firm, yet gentle spring tension. In itself an admirable quality, but that is not all, they are made for a dual purpose. When they are not being worn as earrings they can be worn as finger rings. A deliberate design with fore-thought and direction.

The silver pin by Margaret de Patta incorporates linear bars and geometric shapes, rectangular and circular. The rectangular stones are onyx and agate; the circles are set with colored stones. The two circles are backed with stones of different colors and can be pivoted depending on the costume of the wearer.

Earrings by Irene Brynner. Courtesy of Craft Horizons.   Silver Pin by Margaret de Patta. Photo by F. Boesch.

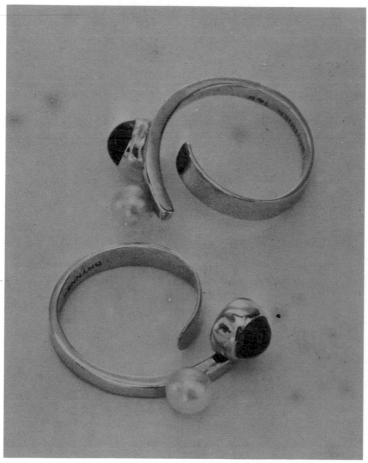

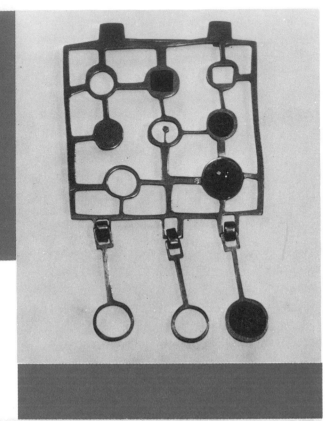

Sterling silver pin, with sawed center design, by Alexandra S. Watkins. Courtesy of the American Craftsmen's Council.

Pierced pin of bronze with three hanging pendants, by Paul S. Mergen. Courtesy of Craft Horizons.

Sterling silver bracelet with sawed out design, by Jean Knutson. Courtesy of the American Craftsmen's Council.

sawed pin

This project emphasizes the use of the saw. The instructions that follow are for a sawed pin with a simple geometric interior design.

Tools:	Saw and blades	**Materials:**	Silver sheet, 18 or 20 gauge
	6″ Hand file		White casein and brush
	Needle files		Solder, #1, #2
	Soldering equipment		Emery cloth
			Flux and brush
			Findings—Catch, joint, and pinstem

1. First clean the metal thoroughly with emery cloth or ammonia solution (ammonia and water). Cover the section to be sawed out with a coat of white casein and allow to dry. Draw your design on paper, then blacken the reverse side with a soft pencil. Using the paper as a carbon, trace the design onto the casein-coated metal. Spray with clear acrylic to keep the design from rubbing off.

2. Saw out the piece to be worked. Remember to hold the saw frame vertically while sawing and to support the metal on the bench pin.

3. If you are planning to make an interior linear design, begin sawing from the outer edge of the work. Do this carefully since the cut made is a fine one and files cannot be used to refine it.

If you are planning on an open shaped interior design (cutting out a negative shape), begin in the same manner but saw along the outline of the shape to be cut out. When sawing is completed, remove the cut out metal. The edges of this design can be refined with needle files if necessary.

4. To finish off the outer edges, file with a 6″ hand file. Remember that files are designed to cut on the away-from-you stroke only. Support the work against the edge of the workbench while filing or hold it in a ring clamp supported by the bench pin.

5. Remove the casein from the metal surface by rubbing it with emery cloth or by placing the cloth on a flat surface and rubbing the metal over it.

6. The piece is now ready to have findings soldered on. First clean the back of the piece since oils from your hands are enough to keep the solder from flowing properly. Polishing with a fine emery cloth is one way of cleaning the surface. To solder findings see page 27.

The findings should be soldered onto the upper third of the piece so that the pin will not flip forward while being worn. For directions on how to rivet a pinstem, see page 32.

7. The pin is complete except for its final polishing. For buffing directions see page 28.

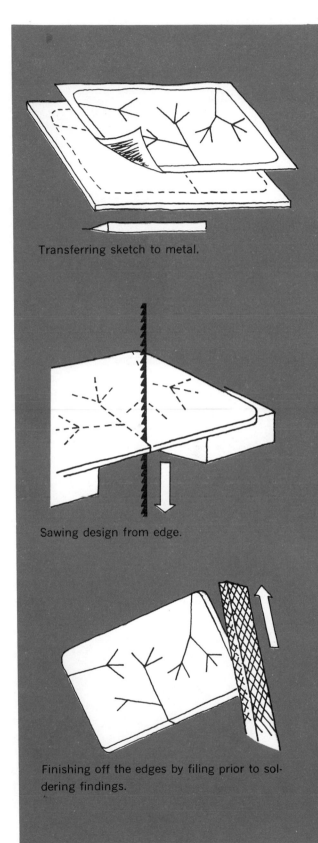

Transferring sketch to metal.

Sawing design from edge.

Finishing off the edges by filing prior to soldering findings.

(Left) Silver pin, sawed wire soldered to oxidized back-plate, by Thomas Gentille. Photograph by Ferdinand Boesch.

(Bottom left) Silver pin with moonstone, pierced and sawed top plate over oxidized forms, by John Prip. Courtesy of the American Craftsmen's Council. Photograph by Renita Hanfling.

(Below) Sterling silver pendant with sawed design and backplate in relief, by F. Jules Reed. Courtesy of the American Craftsmen's Council. Photograph by Anderson.

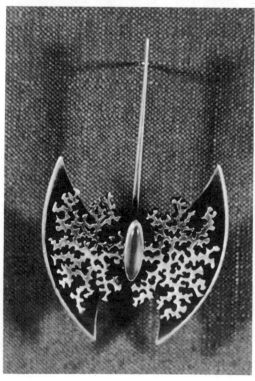

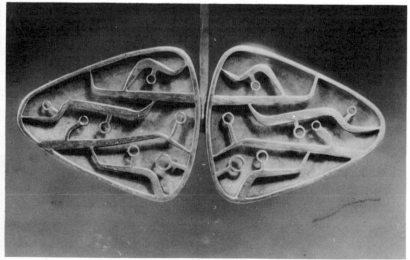

sawed pin with back plate

Although this pin can use the same open shaped design as project #1 it will be quite different in character and color because of the back plate that is used.

Tools:	Saw and blades	**Materials:**	Silver, brass or copper
	6″ Hand file		(6 to 20 gauge—upper plate)
	Ring clamp		(20 gauge—back plate)
	Tweezers		White Casein and brush
	Drill		Solder—#1, #2
	Scriber		Flux and brush
	Soldering equipment		Liver of sulfur
			Tripoli
			Emery cloth

Findings—Catch, joint, and pinstem

1. Begin by drawing your design and transferring it onto the metal as in project #1. Saw out the shape from the metal but do not refine the edges.

2. Next, saw a negative shape from the center of the metal. Pierce the metal and saw along the lines to be cut out. For piercing directions see page 22.

3. Remove the casein and buff the upper surface with tripoli.

4. Now place the piece on a sheet of silver, brass, or copper—this will become the back plate. The same metal as the upper plate may be used or one contrasting to it. With a scriber, draw a light line approximately 1/16″ larger than the upper plate onto the surface of the sheet metal, then saw along this line.

5. Buff the upper surface of the back plate with tripoli.

6. Pickle both pieces to remove all grease in preparation for soldering, neutralize and dry. Place pieces of medium solder (#2) on the back side of the upper plate and sweat solder plates together. For the procedure here see sweat soldering page 26. Pickle again after soldering.

7. Since the upper plate may move slightly during soldering, the back plate is made purposely larger to insure a proper fit after filing. The excess can be filed off with the 6″ hand file. Hold the work in a ring clamp supported against the edge of the workbench. File until both edges are flush and buff with tripoli.

8. The piece is now ready to have the catch and joint soldered on. Use soft solder #1. The pinstem is then inserted and the entire piece buffed.

9. If silver is used for the back plate, it can be oxidized for contrast and for practicality since silver tarnishes. For oxidizing see page 30. After the piece has been oxidized, it receives its final buffing.

Sketch traced on metal

Solder placement on back of upper plate.

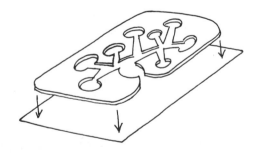

Sawed metal being placed on backplate in preparation for soldering.

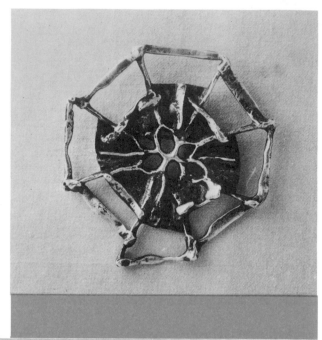

Fused cuff links of sterling silver by Mary Schimpff. Courtesy of Craft Horizons.

Fused silver pin by Lillian F. Kalan. Courtesy of the American Craftsmen's Council. Photograph by Jon Kalan.

Fused silver necklace by Lillian F. Kalan. Courtesy of Craft Horizons. Photograph by Jon Kalan.

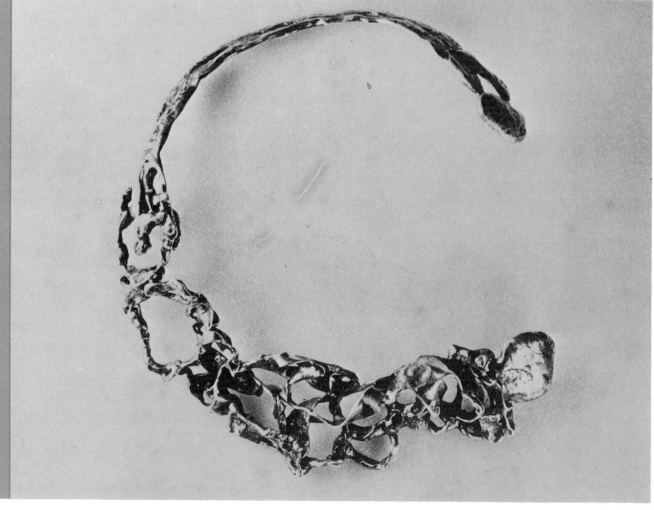

fused pin

Fusing is a method of joining metal by heat without the use of solder. Start with a design concept and within the framework of that concept select, cut, and arrange the metals. They can be bent with the hands or with round nose pliers or twisted into three dimensional forms. Specific shapes can be sawed out and combined with lengths of round and square wire that had been clipped with cutting pliers. Leftover metals can be used or lengths of wire as illustrated.

Tools: Round nose pliers
Scriber
Soldering equipment

Materials: Silver wire
Flux and brush

Findings—Catch, joint,
and pinstem
Solder #1

1. Clean the metals thoroughly and place them on a heating frame over a charcoal block and then onto the pumice pan. Arrange the metals according to your design.

2. Flux the metal liberally.

3. The work is now heated with the torch until it becomes molten and fuses. Part of the excitement in fusing metals is learning how to control the flow of metal, when to bring the torch in closer to heat certain areas, and when to pull it away to cool the metal. While the metal is in a molten state it can be moved about somewhat with the tip of a scriber. The tip must be first heated, otherwise it will cool or possibly freeze the metal.

Gold solder can be added during fusing as a colorant. It will act also as a binding agent.

4. Remove the torch flame and allow the piece to air cool before pickling.

5. The areas in back of the piece that will receive the findings have to be flattened. Use a file or an emery cloth. Solder on the findings with #1 solder, then pickle, neutralize, and buff.

6. Finish off by oxidizing since there will be many low areas and small pits that will tarnish eventually.

7. The final step is to buff off any roughness in the metal as well as any excess oxidation.

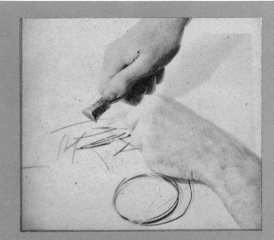
Clipping lengths of wire

Lengths of wire arranged on heating frame and flux added in preparation for fusing.

Joint and catch being positioned for soldering onto the back of the fused pin.

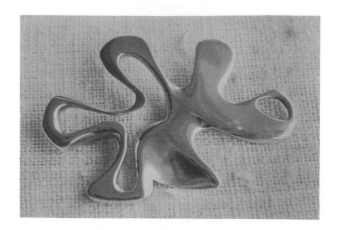

Two pins sawed from 6 gauge sterling silver, then pierced and filed.

Silver cuff links, by Harry Schimpff. The contours here can be achieved with files. Courtesy of the American Craftsmen's Council. Photograph by Ferdinand Boesch.

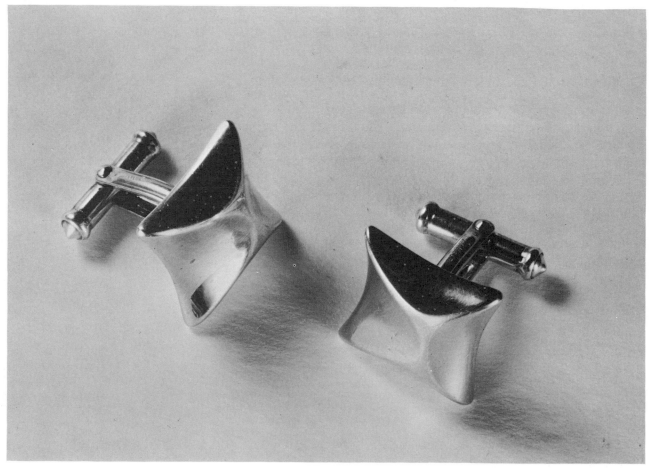

filed pin

Files are used not only to refine forms but to shape them as well. The pin in this project is an example of how a piece can be shaped with files. Remember that files are designed to work on the away-from-you stroke, and it is on this stroke that firm pressure should be exerted.

It is important in this project, as in the others, to recognize that metal is a hard, resistive material and that your forms should be as crisp and hard as the metal itself.

Although the finished piece illustrated here is curvilinear, sharp and angular forms can also be designed. Do not, however, make projections that will stab or tear fine material.

Tools:	Saw and blades	**Materials:**	Silver, copper or brass, 6 gauge
	6″ Hand file		White casein and brush
	Needle files		Beeswax
	Soldering equipment		Flux and brush
			Findings—Catch, joint, and pinstem

1. Begin with an outer shape such as a circle, square, or rectangle and make an interior design that relates to it. Avoid making the design too intricate since needle files are not flexible and cannot reach into small areas.

2. Transfer the design onto the metal and saw out the outer shape. Since the metal is a heavy gauge, use beeswax to lubricate the saw blade, but apply sparingly.

3. When the metal is sawed out, file and shape its contours. This can be done in either of two ways; by following the predetermined design, or by altering it when you sense that the form is taking a new direction. To remove large areas begin the filing with a 6″ half round file or 6″ hand file. Needle files are used for the smaller areas and, since their shapes vary, select those that correspond to the contours you are forming.

4. After you have filed, wrap emery cloth around a stick and remove the file marks. For areas too narrow for the stick to reach, use emery cloth rolled up.

5. Polish the back with emery cloth.

6. Flux the piece well on all sides and solder the findings into position.

7. The pin is now ready to be polished. However in order for the front of the piece to remain sharp and crisp, it should receive as little polishing with the buffing wheel as possible.

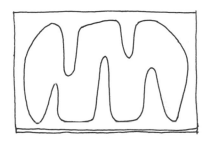

1. Design is traced on metal and outer shape is sawed out. A 6″ hand file is used to remove excess metal around the design.

2. Dotted lines indicate where to shape with needle files.

3. Work showing contours as shaped by files.

Gold ring with filed contours, by Jean Knutson. Courtesy of the American Craftsmen's Council. Photograph by Don Normark.

simple ring

This project will show the simplest way to make a band type ring. Making your first ring can be difficult and some perseverance is required. The silver used is 14 gauge, but if you have difficulty forming this width, use a thinner gauge, such as 20, to practice on first.

Tools:	Saw and blade
	Needle files
	6″ Hand file
	Ring sizes
	Ring Mandrel
	Flat face planishing hammer
	Rawhide mallet
	Flat nose pliers
	Vise
	Soldering equipment
Materials:	Silver, 14 Gauge
	Flux with brush
	Iron binding wire

1. Use ring sizes and select the correct ring size. This size will coincide with the one marked on the ring mandrel.

2. The next step is to determine the length of the metal required. Cut a piece of paper to the planned width of the ring and about 3″ long. Wrap it around the mandrel at the correct size and draw a line at the overlap.

3. Saw a strip of metal to the same length and width as the measured piece of paper.

Liturgical wedding bands in sterling silver by William Frederick. The designs of three bands (upper left, center, and lower right) can be achieved by the split ring method. Courtesy of the American Craftsmen's Council.

4. The metal must be annealed to make it malleable. For annealing directions see page 61. Annealing may be required more than once to bend the ring into position for soldering.

5. Bend the metal by first bending the ends and then the center section over the mandrel. Hold the mandrel in a vise then hammer the metal with a rawhide mallet so that it will bend with a minimum of stretching.

Remove the metal band from the mandrel and with the mallet bend it into a slightly overlapping oval. Do not be afraid to hit the metal. Support the work on the workbench during hammering. Anneal if necessary.

6. The band will have a slight spring tension from the hammering. Pull the overlapping ends apart and release them so that they snap together. Some hammering may be required to make the ends flush. At this stage the ring will be elliptical in shape.

7. The two ends must fit perfectly tight and parallel for soldering. To insure this, saw vertically through the seam where the metal meets. While sawing squeeze the ends tightly together with thumb and forefinger. It may be necessary to saw through the seam several times to insure a perfect fit.

8. Bind with iron binding wire to keep the joint tight during soldering. Check joint by holding it up to the light.

9. Place the ring on a heating frame which is on a pumice pan. Scoop out the pumice from under the frame in order to direct the torch flame from beneath, as well as from above.

10. Flux ring well, and place #1 solder at the top of the seam. Remember that solder will always flow toward the hottest point. Bathe the piece in the torch flame from above as well as from beneath. This will heat the frame also—this is important for if the frame is not completely heated, it will pull heat from the work.

11. After the seam is soldered and the piece has just lost its red color (check in a subdued light) toss it into water to quench. This will keep the metal malleable.

12. Remove iron binding wire. Remember that the wire should never be put into an acid solution as it leaves a copper deposit which can be picked up on future work.

13. Pickle the ring, neutralize, and rinse in running water.

14. To form the ring into a circle, place it on the mandrel and hammer with the rawhide mallet while rotating the mandrel slowly. So that the ring will not be a cone shape, remove it from the mandrel and reverse its position. Repeat hammering until the ring reaches the proper size on the mandrel.

(Continued on next page)

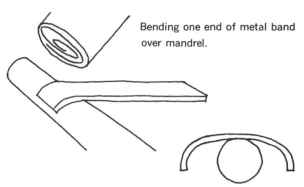

Bending one end of metal band over mandrel.

After both ends are bent, the center section is bent and shaped.

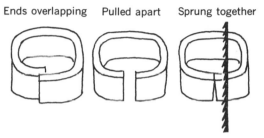

Ends overlapping   Pulled apart   Sprung together

Sawing through joint for alignment

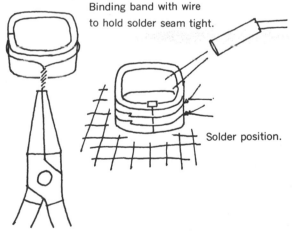

Binding band with wire to hold solder seam tight.

Solder position.

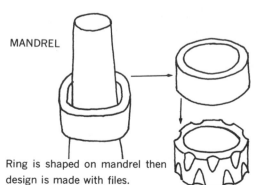

MANDREL

Ring is shaped on mandrel then design is made with files.

A variation of a band ring with champlevé enamel inlay, by John Szymak. Courtesy of the American Craftsmen's Council.

Sterling silver ring with square wire overlay design and black oxidized background, By James E. Frape. Courtesy of Craft Horizons.

15. If the ring is too large, a section of the metal will have to be sawed out, including the solder joint, and the ring resoldered. If the ring is too small, it can be stretched by hammering on the mandrel with the planishing hammer. Rotate during hammering. Anneal if necessary.

16. Make the edges of the ring parallel by placing a 6″ hand file on the workbench and running the ring along its surface. Check the ring to make sure even pressure is being exerted during filing.

17. The design is filed with 6″ files and various needle files. You can file a predetermined design or file directly into the metal and allow forms to develop. A ring clamp can be used to hold the work during filing.

18. Finish off by removing the file marks with emery cloth. The ring can now be oxidized if desired and then polished.

SPLIT RINGS

(Above) Split ring in 18K gold by Carolynn Pence can be made by the split ring method. Courtesy of Craft Horizons. Photograph by Hand Jorgeson. (Right) Split ring, gold with Mexican opal, by Thomas Gentille.

split ring

The split ring will enable you to make a three dimensional design within the band.

Follow all the steps in project #5 except the last one, but use a heavier gauge metal and where solder is called for use #2.

Tools: Saw and blades
Flat nose pliers
6″ Hand file
Scriber
Needle files
Soldering equipment

Materials: Silver, 6 to 12 gauge
Solder #1
Flux with brush
Iron wire binding
Emery cloth

1. Place the ring flat on the workbench, measure the half point and mark it with a scriber. Hold the scriber in position and turn the ring so that a guide line is drawn around its circumference.

2. Saw the ring in half at the guide line while supporting it in the V-shape of the bench pin. Avoid squeezing the ring tightly while sawing as the saw blade can fasten in the seam and break. If this should happen pull the blade out of the ring with flat nose pliers.

3. After the ring has been sawed in half, the rough edges are filed smooth and parallel. To do this place the 6″ hand file on the workbench and run the halves across it.

4. Using various needle files, file the desired design into the edges of the smoothed surfaces.

5. Flux one half of the ring and place pieces of #1 solder at points between the filed areas. Apply heat and melt the solder slightly as in sweat soldering then pickle. File the solder into low flat mounds.

6. Place the two halves of the ring together and bind with iron binding wire to prevent them from slipping during soldering.

7. The ring is now placed on the heating frame and heated until solder flows. Allow it to lose its cherry red color before quenching in water.

8. Remove iron wire and then pickle.

9. Oxidize the ring if desired and buff. To buff the inside of the band, place a felt ring buff on the spindle of the buffing motor and charge with tripoli or use a small buff on the flexible shaft machine.

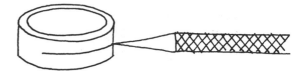

Scribing a guide line for sawing.

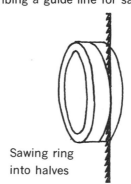

Sawing ring into halves

Design achieved by filing.

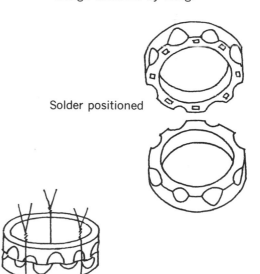

Solder positioned

Halves bound with wire ready for soldering.

Filed areas oxidized then buffed.

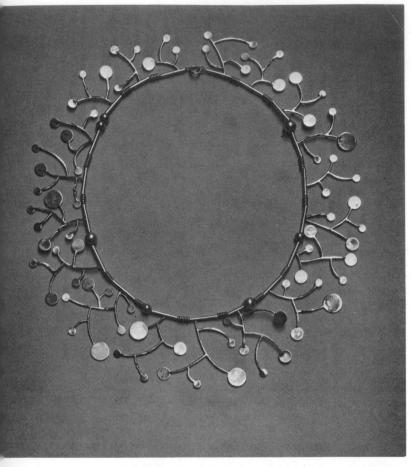

(Left) Gold and silver necklace, branches of gold and discs of silver and gold, by Victor Ries. (Above) Silver cuff link with gold granules on oxidized background, by Ruth S. Roach. Both courtesy of the American Craftsmen's Council.

Pendant with outside forms of silver. The center brass form is set on a black oxidized background.

Bracelet of gold and silver, the circular section uses one metal and the upper forms another, by Sigurd Persson, Sweden. Courtesy of Craft Horizons.

pendant, using mixed metals

Silver, brass, and copper metals solder together readily and all three can be combined in this project. There is also a metal available called Nu-Gold, which is a mixture of brass and copper and has a color very similar to 14K yellow gold.

Various gauges of these metals are sandwiched together and soldered into a block, then sawed or filed to give the piece form. The filing of this block will reveal the different contours and thicknesses of the metals with their rich and subtle color variations.

Tools:	Saw and blades	Materials:	Silver, brass and copper
	Needle files		(various gauges)
	6″ Hand file		Solder #1
	Scriber		Emery cloth
	6″ Round file		Flux and brush
	Soldering equipment		Beeswax

1. Begin by sawing the various gauges of sheet brass, silver and copper into ½″ squares. Saw a sufficient amount so that when stacked they will be 2″ high. The finished piece will measure approximately 2″ x ½″.

2. Arrange the metal for stacking in any sequence you wish, even to staggering the different gauges and metals.

3. Solder together into groups of twos and threes, then pickle. Use #1 solder and sandwich between the metal. It is preferable to use more solder than not enough. After the solder has flowed, it will form a thin band and will appear to be a fine layer of metal.

4. During soldering press with a scriber firmly on the top of each group to bind them together. This pressure will squeeze out excess solder. Heat the scriber point so that it will not absorb heat from the metals.

Continue soldering and pickling until the 2″ height is reached.

5. Since #1 solder is being used, the solder between each metal will melt each time the groups are soldered. This may cause the solder to deteriorate slightly as well as eat into the metals creating small pits.

Even if great care is taken this is difficult to avoid, but the condition can be treated in a few ways: by fluxing the piece and reheating it allowing the solder to flow; by using the small pits or unsoldered areas as starting points for experimentation in the filing of forms; by enlarging the pits with a bur on the flexible shaft machine.

6. Finish off the metal block by rounding its corners with a 6″ hand file. Additional shaping can be accomplished with needle files.

7. Drill a hole in the top area of the piece to permit a cord to be pulled through. Use beeswax to lubricate the drill.

Further development is possible here by sawing out a shape to integrate the drilled hole into the design.

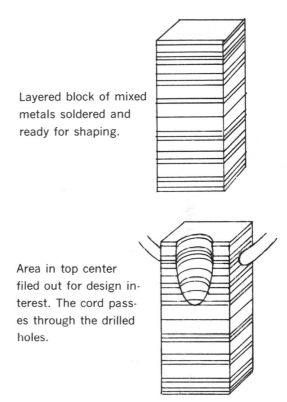

Layered block of mixed metals soldered and ready for shaping.

Area in top center filed out for design interest. The cord passes through the drilled holes.

A. Shape developed by sawing and filing.

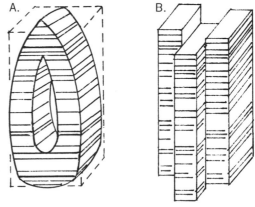

B. Block can be sawed into three sections then resoldered into different positions.

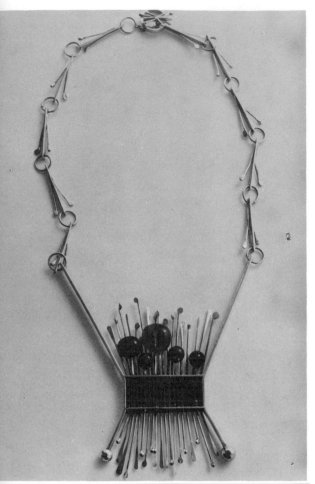

Silver pendant by Arline Fisch. The chain combines forged and constructed metals—some wire ends have been melted so that they ball up. Photograph by Lynn Fayman's Studio. Courtesy of the American Craftsmen's Council.

Winding wire around dowel.

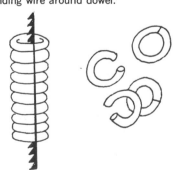

After sawing individual jump rings.

silver chains

THREE VARIATIONS

The three silver chains in this project are composed of individual links which are joined together for flexibility with rings of silver called jump rings. Size specifications can be easily changed to suit individual taste and requirements. The links can vary in width; for example, links worn at the back of the neck can be smaller than those in front or they can stagger in size throughout.

Jump rings are made by winding silver wire tightly around a wooden dowel. One complete turn of the wire will make one ring. To make winding the wire easier, clamp the dowel, including one end of the silver wire, in a vise, or, if the dowel, does not have too large a circumference, hold it and the wire in a ring clamp.

When the wire is completely wound around the dowel, it will resemble a coil. Remove it from the dowel and make a saw cut through each ring. File off any small burrs left on the rings.

Tools:	Saw and blades
	Flat nose pliers
	Round nose pliers
	Cutting pliers
	Planishing hammer
	Steel block
	Drill
	Needle files
	Scriber
	Metal rule
	Soldering equipment
Materials:	Solder, #1, #3
	Flux and brush

CHAIN VARIATION #1—Silver wire, 6 to 14 gauge

1. Clip or saw desired lengths of silver wire.

2. On a steel block, forge the wire to shape with a planishing hammer. See forging, page 61. Forge the ends of each wire wide enough to allow a hole to be drilled. Marks from the forging can be allowed to remain or can be removed with emery cloth.

3. Insert a jump ring into the drilled hole on one end of a link, and then into the hole in another link.

4. Solder the joint of the jump ring with #1 solder, making sure that its ends fit tightly together. During soldering move the forged links away from the solder joint.

5. Repeat the process of adding jump rings to links and then soldering until the chain is completed. The entire piece is pickled and buffed.

CHAIN VARIATION #2—Silver wire 18 Gauge round
Silver sheet metal 18 Gauge

1. To make the individual links, clip lengths of the round wire. The lengths can be anywhere from ½″ to 1½″. It will not be necessary to file the ends flat.

2. Saw 2 bars of silver approximately 3/16″ x ¾″ from the sheet metal. File their edges smooth with a flat edge needle file and buff both pieces.

3. Holes are now drilled along the lengths of the metal, use a drill the same gauge as the wire. A pointed steel bur can also be used. In order to have the holes aligned, place both pieces of metal together in a ring clamp.

4. Insert lengths of precut wire through the drilled holes of both pieces except in one hole at each end, this is where jump rings will be attached to the link. Keep the two bars slightly apart so that the wire will be held in position.

5. Flux well and heat the entire piece, directing the flame along the ends of the wire causing them to melt and ball up. Care must be taken here for although the tendency of the wire is to roll back upon itself as it becomes molten, some of it may drop off resulting in a shorter length link. When the bars are pulled apart the balled wires will keep them from sliding off as they will now be larger than the drilled holes.

Another way of doing this is to follow all the steps up to number 5, then instead of using the torch, support the ends of the wire on a steel block and forge them flat with a planishing hammer.

6. Repeat process until you have the desired number of links. Join the links with round jump rings formed of 18 gauge round silver wire. Insert them into the holes at each end of the links. Flux and solder the joints with #1 solder.

CHAIN VARIATION #3—Silver wire, 10 or 12 gauge round or square.

1. Cut lengths of round or square wire and file their ends flat.

2. For this chain the jump rings and the links will be soldered together. File flat the seam end of a jump ring so that it will fit tightly onto one end of a link. Flux well and solder with hard solder.

3. Solder another jump ring onto a second link but solder the side opposite to the seam leaving the seam side unsoldered.

4. Insert the open end of the second jump ring into the first jump ring. Twist it sideways to open—a pair of round and flat nose pliers can be used—then solder the seam with #1 solder.

5. Repeat process. The individual links can then be polished or they can be filed into various shapes with needle files.

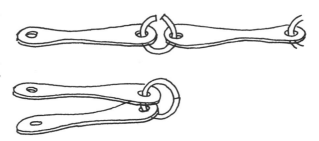

Chain 1. Forged links joined with jump rings. Position for soldering.

Chain 2. Wires inserted through drilled holes. Bars joined with jump rings.

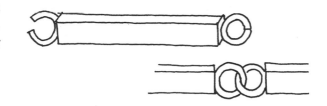

Chain 3. Jump rings soldered to links. Links filed to various shapes.

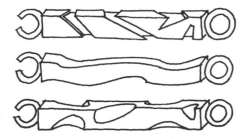

silver comb

There are two practical consideration when designing a comb. The metal must be lightweight and the teeth close enough together so that the comb will not fall out of the hair. The closeness of the teeth will also keep the comb in position while it is being worn.

Solder is not required in this project since the comb teeth are riveted into position. The band on the top part of the comb must be designed to allow for this riveting. Possible designs for the ornamented top section are offered in the diagrams.

Tools:	Saw and blades	Materials:	Silver wire, round, 14 or 16 gauge
	Drill		Silver sheet, 20 gauge
	Needle files		Emery cloth
	Scriber		
	Planishing hammer		
	Steel block		

1. Rub the back of the drawing with a pencil and trace directly onto 20 gauge silver sheet. For further clarity, incise the tracing with a scriber.

2. Using the scribed line as a guide, saw the shape from the silver.

3. Place the sawed metal on a steel block and hammer its entire surface with the flat end of a planishing hammer. The hammer and steel block must be kept clean since dust or foreign matter can become imbedded in the silver during hammering. They can be wiped clean with the palm of the hand when work begins and from time to time as work proceeds.

The hammering will give a lightly textured surface to the metal. This texture can be developed or removed depending upon its appearance. Hammering also tends to stretch the metal slightly out of shape, but this is corrected by changing the direction and pressure of the blows.

4. The teeth can now be forged of 14 or 16 gauge round wire. A minimum of two teeth, at least 5″ long, are necessary to hold the comb in the hair. When more teeth are used, they can be of a shorter length, but they should extend at least 2″ from the edge of the upper section.

The teeth must be designed to fulfill these requirements:
    a. The upper ends of the wire must be flattened so that they can be riveted flush to the comb, and they must be wide enough so that a small hole can be drilled to accommodate the rivet.
    b. The lower ends of the wire must slide easily into the hair but must not be too pointed, and they must hold the comb in position.

5. After the wire is forged the ends can be filed with needle files to refine them and to give them the desired shape. Remove file marks, as well as forging marks, with emery cloth if you so desire.

Comb, silver and brass, by Vera Allison. Photograph by R. Randolph. Courtesy of the American Craftsmen's Council.

Sawed design for comb with two variations for attaching prongs.

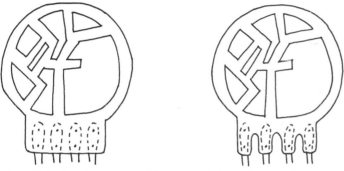

Pierced design for comb with two variations for attaching prongs.

Two variations of prongs

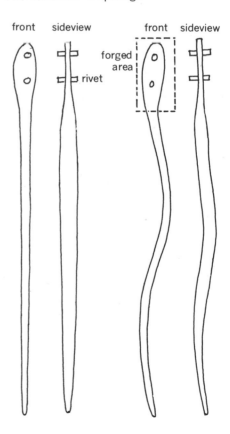

6. The teeth can now be riveted to the upper section of the comb. They should be placed high enough to allow for a minimum of two rivets for each tooth. This amount will keep the teeth from pivoting and will give additional support.

7. First drill the holes for the rivets. To insure a tight fit, the drill must be the same gauge as the silver that will be used for the rivets.

The upper section of the comb and the teeth must be held together during drilling so that the holes will be aligned. The work can be placed in a ring clamp and supported against the bench pin or it can be placed on the workbench and pressed down into position with the fingers.

8. When all the holes have been drilled, put the rivets through and hammer them down. This is done in the same manner as riveting a pin-stem, see page 32. Directions for making the rivets will be found there also.

9. The teeth can be bent slightly with the fingers to fit the shape of the head. The work is then buffed.

Gold brooch with pearls by Reinhold Reiling, Germany. Courtesy of Craft Horizons.

(Above) Gold pin with opal. (Below) silver pin with pearl. Both by Miye Matsukata. Courtesy of Craft Horizons.

gold pin with stone

This project is a fabrication of a gold wire pin with a bezel-mounted stone. There is no backplate and the work, depending on the design, can be quite open.

Since there are a great many solder joints yellow ochre is used to prevent the solder from flowing in already soldered joints.

Tools: Saw and blades
Cutting pliers
Flat needle file
Half round needle file
Round nose pliers
Ring clamp
Tweezers
Burnisher
Soldering equipment

Materials: 14K Yellow gold wire, round (16 gauge)
Solder—14K yellow gold (soft, medium, hard)
Stone—Flat bottom cabochon
Gold bezel wire
22 gauge 14K sheet metal
Yellow ochre

1. In order to know the length of wire required draw your design on paper and add an inch or two to allow for the amount taken up in the sawing and filing of the wire.

2. Clip or saw lengths of wire using your drawing as a pattern but allow approximately 1 or 2 millimeters extra to each. If your design calls for complex curved lengths of wire, shape them with the round nose pliers. If the curve is a simple one run the burnisher along the lengths of wire causing it to curve.

3. File the ends of the wire at the correct angles to insure a proper fit for soldering. Use a flat needle file. The wire is supported in the ring clamp with about 2mm. extending from the jaws.

4. Each wire is dipped in flux and with tweezers placed in position, according to your design, on a smooth charcoal block in the pumice pan.

5. Add additional flux at each joint and heat slightly until flux is just dry. Place fluxed #2 solder (medium) at each juncture.

6. Solder in subdued light so you can watch the work closely—the wire is fine and can melt easily. Begin heating slowly so that, until the flux causes them to adhere, the small pieces of solder will not blow away. Bring the torch closer and allow solder to flow. If the torch flame is able to engulf the entire piece, all the solder will flow at approximately the same time; otherwise aim the torch covering groups of junctures at a time, allow the solder to flow and move quickly to adjoining areas. Quench and pickle.

7. A collar bezel is now made and its joint soldered with #3 solder. See bezels, page 31.

8. Next a base of metal upon which the stone can rest must be made and inserted into the bezel. It will be soldered to the wire structure later. First insert the stone in the bezel to hold the bezel in position. Place both on 22 gauge gold sheet metal and scribe a light line around the bezel onto the metal surface. Remove the stone, saw out the base accurately as the fit must be perfect, file the edges smooth being careful not to remove too much metal.

9. Pierce the center of the base with a drill for the insertion of a saw blade and saw out the center area leaving a ring of metal. 2mm. width is sufficient. This space will permit light to pass through a transparent stone. Ideally the rim should be of gold, however, since it will not be seen, except from the back, silver, brass, or copper can also be used.

10. To solder, insert the base into the bezel and place on heating frame. Flux well. Place small pieces of #2 solder on the base where it touches the bezel. Heat the entire piece, then direct the torch flame from underneath so that solder will flow down into the seam and not up onto the bezel. This will also prevent the fine bezel wire from melting. Allow the piece to just lose its red color and quench in pickle, this will keep the bezel malleable.

11. Place the soldered gold wire form on a flat charcoal block and place the bezel in position on the form. Since the bezel base and the gold wires have been soldered with #2 solder, coat the wire juncture as well as the inside seams of the bezel with yellow ochre to prevent the solder from reflowing. If the bezel rests on a juncture do not cover the juncture with the ochre (see yellow ochre page 33). Then solder, quench, and pickle.

12. The piece is now ready to have findings soldered on. First file the area flat to make a base for the findings, removing as little metal as necessary since the wire is quite thin. Place the work upside down on the charcoal block allowing the bezel to hang over the side, and supporting it with pumice if necessary. Place the findings on a juncture, if possible, so that they will not show from the front. Use #1 solder. Flux the entire piece and heat it until the flux becomes transparent. Aim torch in the area where the findings are and solder them in place one at a time. Allow the piece to air cool slightly before pickling. This will give the wire strength.

13. Put the stone into the bezel and push the bezel into position around the stone. Rivet the pinstem into place.

14. The piece is now polished. Since the work is fine, care must be exercised during buffing. Do not buff the stone directly, it can be protected with masking or transparent tape.

DESIGN VARIATIONS

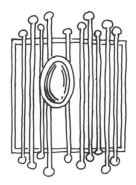

Vertical pin—wires with balled ends.

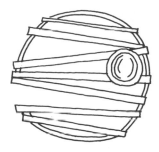

Circular pin—wires placed diagonally over circular frame.

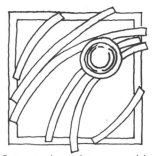

Square pin—wires curved by forging.

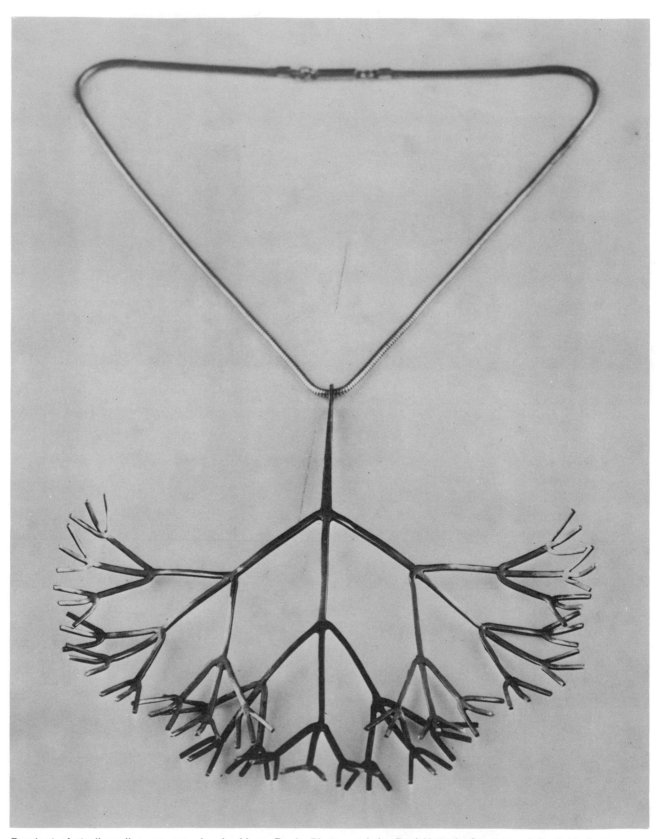

Pendant of sterling silver square wire, by Merry Renk. Photograph by Paul Hassel. Courtesy of Craft Horizons.

forging

Forging refers to the shaping and forming of metal with the use of special hammers and stakes. By handling the jewelry metals the craftsman learns how workable they are and how this workable quality can be employed.

Stakes, hammers, and the metal being forged must be kept clean and are wiped with the palm of the hand before and during forging. Dust that becomes imbedded in the metal is difficult to remove.

Annealing

During the forging process of hammering and stretching, metal becomes hardened to a point where it will fatigue and crack unless its molecular structure is softened. This hardening can be corrected by annealing the metal, that is by heating it to a deep cherry red color, allowing it to cool until the color is just gone, and quenching it in water. It is then pickled to remove flux and fire scale. The metal can also be quenched directly in the pickle.

Annealing may be done before forging begins. The work is covered with flux to help prevent fire scale and is then heated with the torch. It should be kept in mind that the color of metal is best seen in subdued light. If more stretching of the metal is required, annealing can be repeated as necessary.

Forging on a Block

A beginner will not find it difficult to forge simple shapes and can practice with a 10 to 18 gauge silver wire. The only tools required are a flat face planishing hammer and a steel block. One end of the metal is supported on the steel block and hammered until it is flattened and broadened, beginning at the center and working towards the outside edges. The uneven edges are then filed to obtain a smooth contour.

Several pieces can be forged in this way; after the pieces have been forged to shape they can be soldered together in different combinations with #2 solder to make simple, yet elegant, pieces of jewelry. Findings can then be soldered in place with #1 solder. After final soldering, the piece is air cooled before being cleaned in acid. Air cooling will keep the metal hard and in tension.

Forging on a Stake

A variety of hammers and stakes are used to form the metal into various shapes and contours. The stakes are chosen to follow the curves of the design accurately as the work must be supported at all times during hammering. The hammers also are chosen for shape, each shape moving the metal in a different direction.

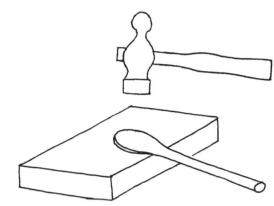

Forging one end of round wire on a steel block.

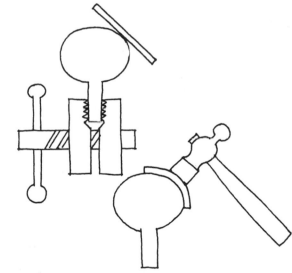

Forging metal to shape on steel stake.

Metal can be forged to various shapes by using the correct stakes.

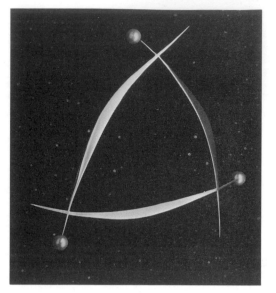

With practice you will be able to determine which hammer will best shape the metal in the desired direction, and the amount of control to exercise in directing the blows. Brute force is not required in forging, rather a rhythmical precise series of blows is maintained so that the metal will not be thick in some areas and thin in others. A wire and sheet gauge which measures the thickness of the metal is used frequently during forging.

To form a bowl shape, a round flat sheet of metal is placed on the stake and hammering is begun at the center, spiraling around in even uniform blows to the edge of the metal. This is repeated several times. Annealing will then be necessary. The hammering is repeated and alternated with annealing until the desired form is achieved.

If the final form is quite complex or the curves cannot be forged from one piece of metal, separate sections are forged and then soldered together.

(Top) Silver pin by Hazel E. Sweeney. Photograph by Louis Mervar.

(Right) Forged watch bracelet of 18K gold with light and dark-colored topaz. The light-colored topaz is placed over the watch. By Irene Brynner. Courtesy of Craft Horizons.

(Bottom) Bracelet with forged silver shapes, by Arline Fisch. Courtesy of Craft Horizons.

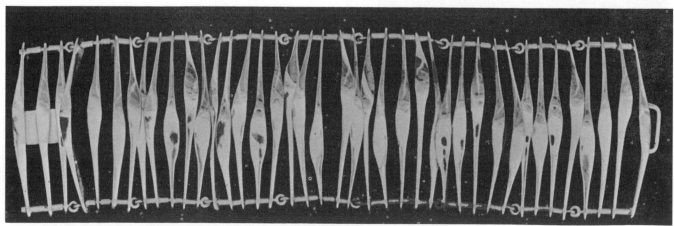

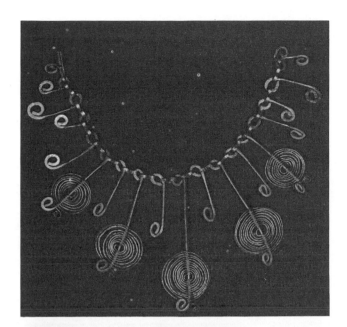

(Left) Forged sterling silver necklace, by Nancy Cohen. Courtesy of The Cleveland Museum of Art.

(Below) Forged necklace, silver with constructed pendant set with a citrine, by Frank Patania, Jr. Courtesy of Craft Horizons.

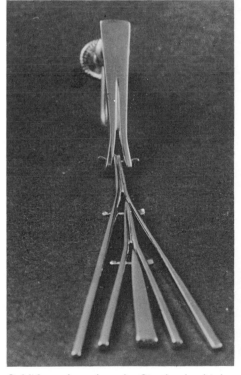

Gold forged earrings by Stanley Lechtzin.

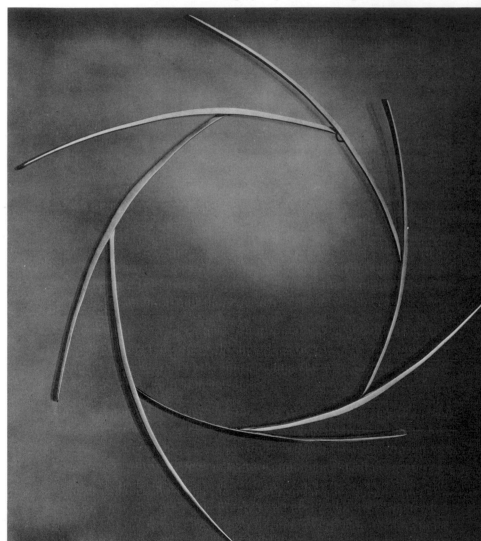

Forged sterling steel flexible spoke necklace, by Betty Cooke. Courtesy of the American Craftsmen's Council. Photograph by James K. Lightner.

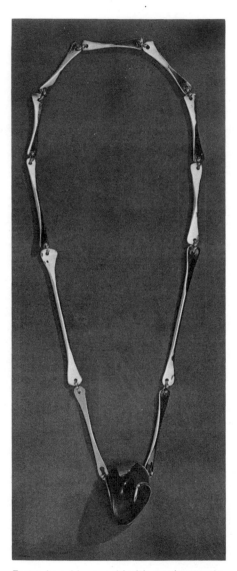

Forged necklace, gold with smoky quartz, by Shirley Lege Carpenter. Courtesy of the American Craftsmen's Council. Photograph by John Rogers.

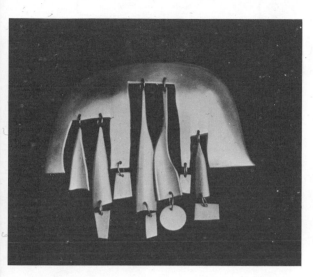

Forged silver pin using jump rings, by Dorothy S. Benrimo. Courtesy of Craft Horizons. Photograph by Joseph Baum.

Forged gold necklace with gold, blue and green colored Inca beads, by Mary Fisher Traver. Hallmark Award. Courtesy of Craft Horizons.

Forged bracelets with etched silver, gold, and areas of oxidation, by Margery Anneberg. Courtesy of Craft Horizons. Photograph by Hawkin.

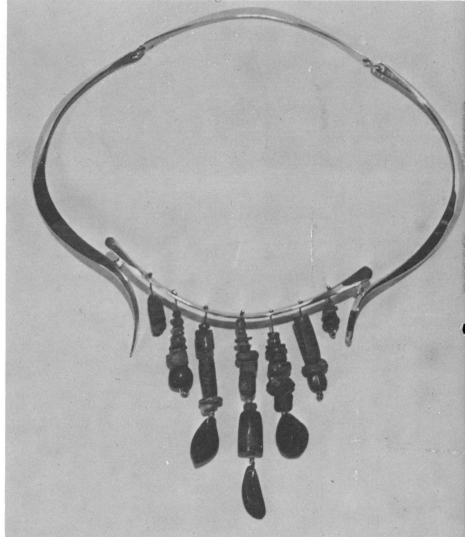

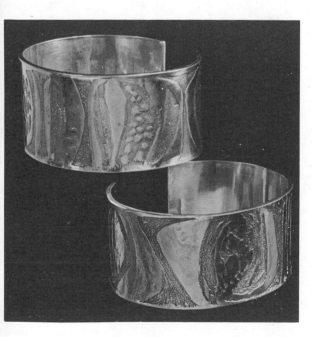

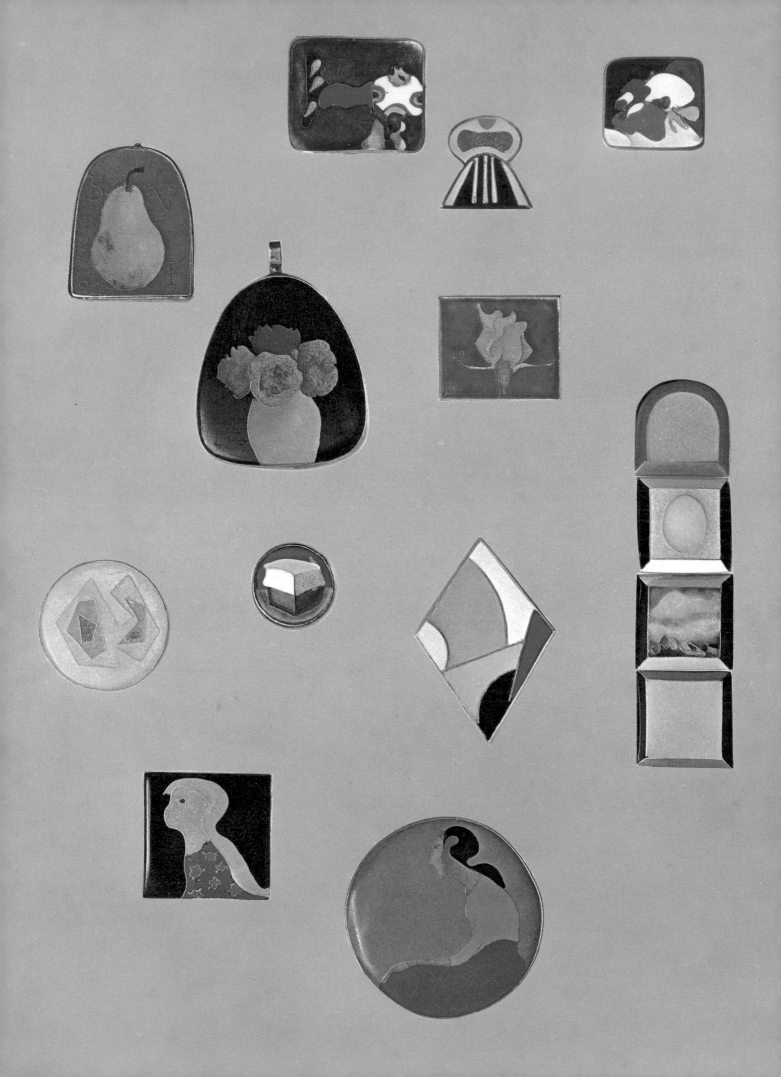

enameling

Enameling is a method of applying finely ground powdered glass onto a metal surface. When heated, the enamel will melt and fuse to the metal to produce richly colored pieces of jewelry.

The three types of enamels—opaque, translucent or transparent, and opalescent—come in a wide variety of colors and can be purchased ground to various degrees of fineness. Since the colors are often completely different after being fired and also change when fired over different metals, test samples should be made to determine the fired quality of each enamel.

The metals, generally copper, fine silver, and gold, are cleaned with emery cloth and pickled in a nitric acid solution. The enamels are washed until all impurities and milky residues are rinsed away. They can then be placed in jars and labeled or used wet.

The enamel wetted to its saturation point is laid on with a spatula. A pointer places it in position, and a spreader flattens it to a uniform depth. During this process it is sprayed with a weak gum tragacanth solution kept in an atomizer. This keeps the enamel damp and acts as a bonding agent. The enamel is then allowed to dry completely before being placed in a hot kiln. On flat pieces of metal, the reverse side is also enameled (referred to as counterenameling) to prevent the enamel from cracking while cooling since metal expands and contracts more than glass.

Of the several enameling techniques, three will be discussed here—cloisonné, plique-à-jour, and champlevé.

Cloisonné

In cloisonné, from the French cloison, meaning "partition," each color is enclosed within a wire partition soldered onto a backplate. The backplate is cut from sheet metal, gold is best as it can be brought to maximum heat repeatedly without apparent oxidizing whereas silver and copper turn black, and the oxidation is difficult to remove. The metal is rubbed with coarse steel wool, since enamel does not adhere well to a smooth surface, and then cleaned in a nitric acid solution.

Thin wires of fine gold are placed onto the plate, according to design, and are soldered into position. The enamel is laid into the areas formed by the walled partitions, or cloisons, and fired in a kiln. With the first firing the enamel will shrink; more enamel should be added and fired until the level of the wires is reached. A Carborundum stone is rubbed on the enamel to remove any excess, and the piece is fired.

An alternate method of making cloisonné, is one in which solder is not used. A gum tragacanth solution is mixed to a glue consistency and when hardened holds the wires in place while the enamels are applied. Once the piece is fired the enamel, wires, and backplate all fuse together.

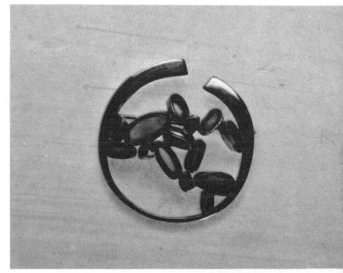

Pin in 14K gold and plique-à-jour enamel, by Polly Stehman. Courtesy of the American Craftsmen's Council.

(Opposite page) A selection of cloisonné enamels from Robert Kulicke's workshop which were designed by a group of painters and executed by craftsmen. Top row, (left to right) two pins by RON GORCHOV, executed by URSULLA LINGER and MEEKEE LEE, and a pin designed and made by DEVON MEADE. Second row, two pendants by ROBERT KULICKE, the pear executed by KULICKE, the flowers by ALICE FRANKEL, and a yellow rose pin designed and made by DUNY KATZMAN. Third row, (left) a pin by MON LEVINSON, executed by DORIS FREEDMAN, next to it WAYNE THIEBAUD's pie pin, executed by DUNY KATZMAN, a pin by KNOX MARTIN, executed by JUDY SHAW, and a group of four enamels designed and executed by MIRIAM SHAPIRO. Bottom row two pins by HERB KATZMAN, the child made by KATZMAN and the seated woman by KULICKE. Photograph by Louis Mervar. Courtesy of Craft Horizons.

Shown here are the master drawing with color notations, the flower pendant with the cloisons shaped and placed on the backplate, some of the tools used, and the finished enamel.

Plique-à-jour

Plique-à-jour is similar to cloisonné, but there is no backplate, and transparent colors are used.

There are several ways to do plique-à-jour, and this is one. Wires of fine gold are bent to shape, then soldered together and placed on a sheet of mica. The individual cloisons must be small. This will add support and strength to the piece as well as give it a jewel-like quality. The enamel is placed in the cloisons and fired until it reaches the level of the wires. After the final firing, the mica is removed, leaving a panel of enamel through which light can pass producing an effect very similar to stained glass.

Champlevé

In champlevé, or inlaid enameling, cloisons are formed by recessing areas of the metal surface. This can be done by punching or carving the metal to form the individual cells, but the method most used today is to recess the areas in an acid solution. The areas not to be lowered are protected with asphaltum, and the technique is the same as etching, see page 34. The surface should be eaten away 1/50″ or one-half the thickness of the metal.

Once the piece is etched, the asphaltum is removed, and the cells are filled with enamel and fired. Enamel is added and firing is repeated until the level of the metal surface is reached. Both metal and enamel are stoned with Carborundum to give a smooth flat surface. The work is then refired and buffed with tripoli.

THE FOLLOWING SERIES OF PHOTOGRAPHS DEMONSTRATES THE STEPS IN CLOISONNE ENAMELING.

1. Bending the cloisonné wires over the master drawing.

2. Transferring the wires to the metal plate with tweezers.

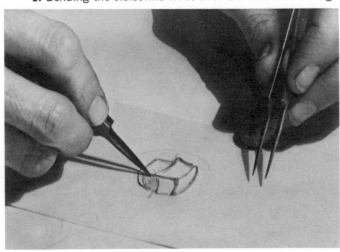

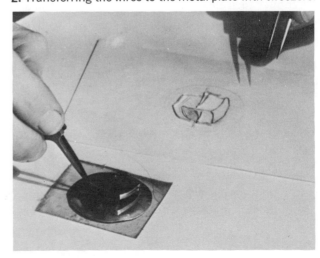

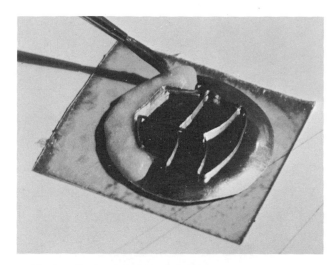

3. Placing first enamel in cloison.

4. Filling in remaining areas with enamel.

5. Work placed on top of kiln to dry.

6. Enamel placed in heated kiln for firing.

7. Enamel set in heated pitch on dop stick, in preparation for polishing.

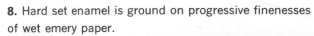

8. Hard set enamel is ground on progressive finenesses of wet emery paper.

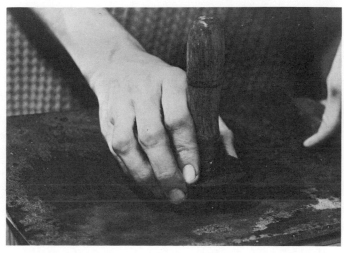

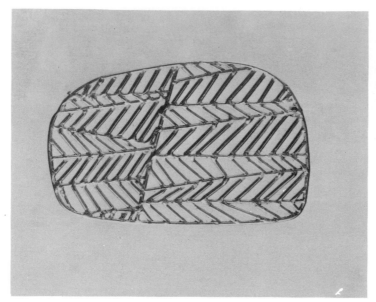

Cast gold pin, and gold earrings, by Thomas Gentille. Photographs by Ferdinand Boesch.

Necklace, cast in sections, silver with iron pyrite crystals, by Alice Shannon.
Courtesy of the American Craftsmen's Council. Photograph by F. Boesch.

casting

Lost wax is the classic form of casting. Although used for many centuries primarily for the casting of bronze sculpture, it has become, within the past decade, more of a jewelry technique.

Making the Wax Model

Casting waxes vary in hardness and melting properties. Dental wax, a medium hard wax which does not melt at body temperature, is excellent and can be used alone or in combination with other waxes. Dental wax (which comes in sheets and rods of various shapes) can be used as a base with a softer pliable wax worked over it for textural interest. Every detail of the wax reproduces exactly in the metal.

After the wax model is made the sprue and vents, also of wax, are added. The sprue is the area through which the molten metal will flow. The vents allow gasses to escape when the metal is poured in and during the heating of the investment.

A metal sprue cone is placed on the sprue and attached in place with wax. Its shape, similar to a funnel without the long end, provides a large area through which to pour the metal.

When the sprue and vents are in place the piece is coated with a liquid debubblizer. A sable brush can be used for this. Debubblizer helps the investment adhere to the wax model and also prevents small bubbles from forming on the surface of the piece during casting.

The Investment

Investment is a mixture of clay, grog, and plaster which renders it porous and enables it to be fired in a kiln. It can be purchased commercially prepared.

A small amount of investment is coated onto the wax model, with a watercolor brush. The purpose of this initial coating is to insure that all areas of the model are covered. The piece is turned upside down and placed into a ring or flask of metal which then has its bottom rim sealed with clay to keep the investment from seeping out. The flask can be made of a length of pipe, or can be purchased in various sizes. Galvanized pipe should not be used as it will produce dangerous fumes when heated. For the small bird shape shown here, or for a ring, a length of pipe with a 2½″ diameter by 3″ length is sufficient. Since the metal is in a molten state and creates tremendous pressure when poured, the flask should always be larger than the piece to allow for any expansion of the investment, and the piece should not be more than ½″ from the top of the flask. Vents reduce this pressure by allowing gasses to escape and the ingredients in the investment help also. If the investment should develop serious cracks, the metal may be lost into these cracks and the piece lost as well. Sometimes there are narrow cracks in the investment and a small quantity of metal escapes. These areas, called flashings, can be filed off after the piece is cast.

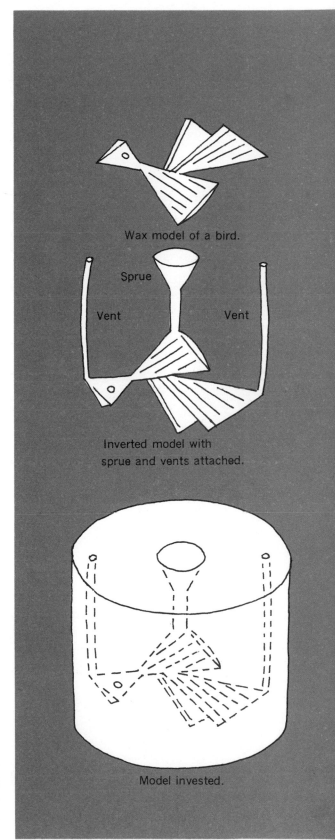

Wax model of a bird.

Sprue

Vent　　　Vent

Inverted model with sprue and vents attached.

Model invested.

The flask with the wax piece inside is filled to the top with the investment and the investment allowed to dry. Light taps repeated on the flask with a metal scribe handle or other tool will bring air bubbles to the surface and prevent the investment from building up pressure that will cause it to crack when fired.

After the investment has set, it is leveled with a flat metal edge run across its surface and allowed to dry—this can take from 8 to 12 hours. The drying time for a large sculptured piece can be a week to 10 days or longer. Once the investment has dried the metal sprue cone is removed.

Burnout

The investment is placed, sprue opening down, into a kiln which is at room temperature. The kiln is then turned on low, heating the investment slowly. The investment can be supported on stilts or against a piece of asbestos so that the wax will flow out easily and burn away completely.

During this heating period the investment will become bone dry and the wax will flow or burn out. Hence the term "lost wax." The burnout can take approximately 4 to 5 hours.

Casting the Model

The piece is removed from the kiln while red hot with a pair of steel tongs and placed directly into the centrifugal machine.

The centrifugal machine is spring activated. When the spring is released, molten metal is forced into the cavity left by the burnout. The machine should be bolted down securely to a table and encircled with a protective shield made of galvanized sheet metal.

Cast gold wedding rings; the larger ring is oxidized a deep brown, the smaller one is pierced, by Thomas Gentille. Photograph by Ferdinand Boesch.

The crucible is fitted against the mouth of the investment. The metal (which has been pickled to remove all dirt and grease) is put into the crucible and melted with an acetylene torch until it resembles mercury and moves easily when the arm of the machine is shaken gently. It must not be overheated or allowed to boil. Any impurities will rise to the surface and can be removed with a flattened piece of coat hanger wire (minus its paint). A pinch or two of powdered borax, which acts as a flux, is added to help the metal begin to flow and added again just before the spring is released. In a simultaneous action the flame is withdrawn from the molten metal and the spring released, forcing the molten metal into the areas of the lost wax.

The correct amount of metal required for casting the piece can be determined by the water displacement method. First the wax model is submerged in a small glass container filled about ¾ with water and the raised level of water marked on the outside of the glass. Remove from container and add metal until water reaches level mark. To this more metal is added, at least ¼ of the total amount.

Removing Investment

The flask with the cast piece inside is removed from the centrifugal machine with steel tongs.

When the metal has cooled and lost its cherry red color, which is best seen in a subdued light, it is plunged into a bucket of cold water. If the metal is not allowed to cool the shock of the cold water could cause the investment to explode or the metal to become grainy in texture. Even though the metal has lost its red color, it and the investment will still be hot enough to cause much sputtering and splashing of water. This is as it should be; the investment is breaking up.

It will take a few minutes, before the investment is cool enough to handle. Most of it will have fallen out of the flask, and the remainder can be poked out with a short length of wire. This should be done carefully so that the piece will not be damaged. Any remaining investment can be scrubbed off under running water with a toothbrush.

Finishing the Piece

The sprue and vents, which have been also filled or partially filled with metal, are clipped off from the piece and filed down. The piece can now be polished, have findings attached, stones set, be oxidized, or finished in any way desired.

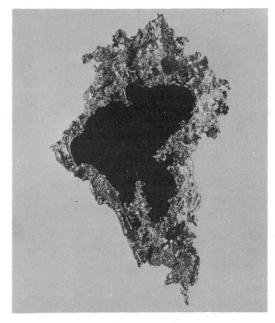

Cast pin of 18 K gold with turquoise by Hans Krahmer. Courtesy of the American Craftsmen's Council. Photograph by Ferdinand Boesch.

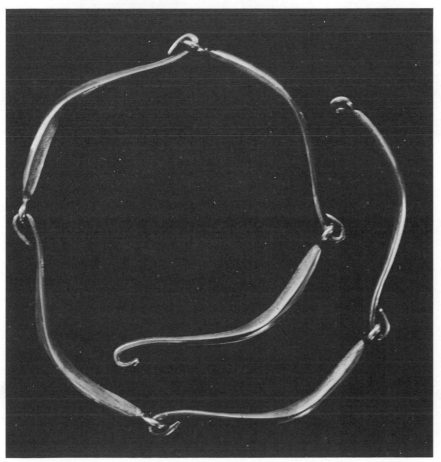

Sand cast necklace of sterling silver, by Richard C. Gompf. Courtesy of the American Craftsmen's Council. Photograph by Anne Petray.

Lost Wax Casting

The following series of photographs demonstrates the steps in lost wax casting after the wax model has been invested: the burnout, casting the model, removing the investment, and finishing the piece.

1. If metal sprue cone is not used excess investment is removed from the opening.

2. Investment placed, sprue opening down, into kiln with space allowed for wax to run out.

3. Wax burning out in kiln.

4. After the spring of the centrifugal machine has been wound, a peg is placed to hold it in position.

5. Metal being placed in crucible of centrifugal machine. Leftover metal may be used.

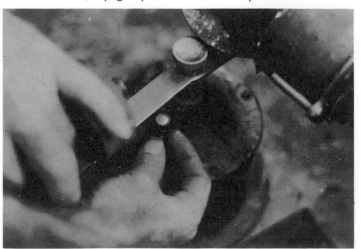

6. Hot investment is positioned in centrifugal machine and crucible is fitted against mouth of investment.

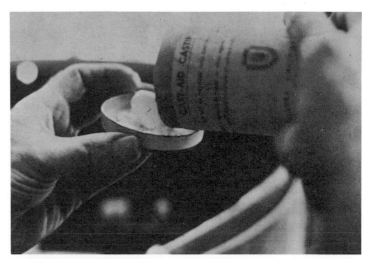

7. Powdered borax being added to metal.

8. Metal heated to molten state, prior to release of spring mechanism.

9. After casting, the investment is plunged into cold water where it partially disintegrates.

10. The sprues are removed.

11. The piece is then oxidized.

12. Finish by buffing.

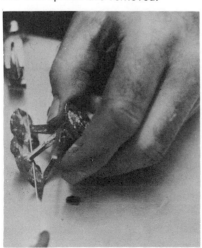

Gold pendant with granulation, Byzantine, 10th century. Courtesy of The Cleveland Museum of Art

Brooch of 18K gold with granulation, "Seed" by John Paul Miller. Courtesy of the American Craftsmen's Council.

granulation

Granulation, the art of fastening gold granules onto another body of gold without the use of solder, reached its height of excellence during Hellenistic times. There were sporadic attempts at duplicating this highly skilled technique during the centuries that followed, but the old records of the period contained information that was vague and measurements that were for the most part arbitrary.

The challenge continued, however, until today there are a few leading craftsmen who are doing granulation, either by having rediscovered the process or by having developed their own. The writings of Pliny the Elder (23–79 A.D.), a Roman author, have been of some help in supplying clues to the original methods used. At present there are several possible ways of working this technique.

Making the small granules, or grains as they are also called, is relatively simple. They are prepared by clipping small pieces of gold from wire or from sheet metal which are then melted by being suspended in powdered charcoal. This is done by putting the pieces into a crucible which already contains a layer of powdered charcoal; the gold pieces are then alternated with further layers of charcoal until the crucible is filled. The crucible with its contents can then be heated with a torch or put into a kiln.

After the heating is completed, and the gold has melted, the crucible is allowed to cool. The granules will be perfectly spherical at this point since grains of gold heated to the melting point draw up into themselves to form spheres and remain in this shape even upon cooling. The contents of the crucible are then emptied into a pan of water. Since the granules are heavier than the charcoal, they will drop to the bottom of the pan which will allow the charcoal to be removed easily.

The granules can be sorted by being sifted through various fine mesh screens and then stored by size in jars for easy identification.

Fastening the granules to the gold base work which has already been prepared takes place when they are both heated. One method is to first pick up the granules with a fine pointed sable brush which has been dipped in a gum solution. They can be picked up one at a time, or in clusters, and then moved about once they are placed on the base work. The gum solution will hold or glue the granules in position and prevent them from rolling off. Unless the gold contains a high enough percentage of copper, a copper salt can be mixed with the gum solution. Copper lowers the melting temperature of gold.

Both the gold base work and the granules are heated with a reducing flame (which shows a great deal of yellow and will not melt the metal as quickly as other flames) until the skins on their surfaces become fastened through a molecular exchange and bind together at the point of contact.

Gold ring with granulation, by Stanley Lechtzin. Courtesy of Craft Horizons.

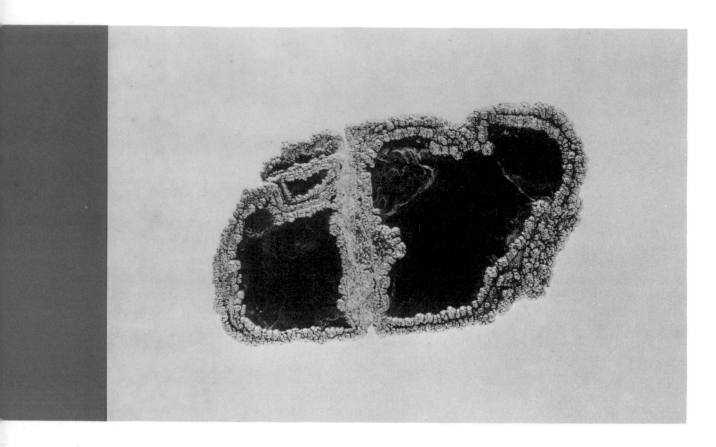

Three pieces by Stanley Lechtzin: (Above) Gilded silver pin, electroformed with mica as its stone. (Right) Silver and field-stone pendant, electroformed over a styrofoam and fieldstone matrix. (Below) Gold plated silver pin, electroformed over a styrofoam matrix.

electroforming

Recently there have been several contributions to the jewelry craft, but, as important as these are, they are minimal compared to the more recent contribution of electroforming. The experimentation in electrochemistry began with the English physicist Michael Faraday in the early 19th century, but only within the last several years has electrofabrication been successfully applied to jewelry through the experimentation of Stanley Lechtzin.

The procedure of electroforming is extremely technical and is not intended for the beginner craftsman. It is included in this text because of its recent and important contribution to the jeweler.

CAUTION: The reader is cautioned that cyanide, which is used here, is very poisonous in any form. It should be kept in mind that if acid comes in contact with cyanide, deadly hydrocyanic gas is produced.

Electroforming is the art of building metallic pieces by electrodeposition on a base or matrix, which is then removed in whole or in part, leaving a shell of electrodeposited metal. Electrodeposition requires a direct current source and a solution, usually a water solution of metallic salts. The current can be supplied by dry cells or, more practically, by an electroplating rectifier, a device which changes the alternating current to direct current. Rectifiers are also equipped with rheostats which enable varying the voltage from less than 1 volt to more than 10 volts.

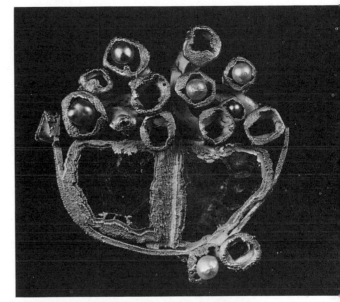

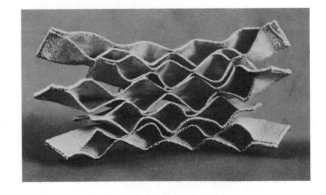

(Top) Silver gilt pin with mica and pearls, electroformed over a matrix of wax. (Below) Another example of an electroformed silver gilt pin, both by Stanley Lechtzin.

There are two basic types of electroplating solutions in use; acid solutions and cyanide solutions. The process, in its simplest form, consists in passing direct current between two electrodes immersed in a metallic-salt solution. A positive electrode (anode) supplies an electron which passes from it to the negative electrode (cathode) which is the work being formed, and is there deposited—the electron flow always being from anode to cathode and in a straight line. Therefore, more metal can be expected to be deposited on the high metal areas of the matrix, which are called high current density areas. Anodes are attached to stainless steel hooks which are passive and do not go into solution.

Where agitation is called for in a bath, it can be supplied by a magnetic laboratory stirring device which is ideal for agitation as it does not take up tank space and its speed is easily controlled.

The baths require constant filtration, for which an aquarium filter can be used. This filters the bath through layers of glass fiber, removing suspended matter, and activated carbon, which removes organic contamination. The latter, if allowed to accumulate, would impair the bath's function. There is, then, a need for extreme cleanliness and the

Equipment and arrangement for electroforming as developed by Stanley Lechtzin.

Closeup of acid copper bath.

Closeup of silver forming bath.

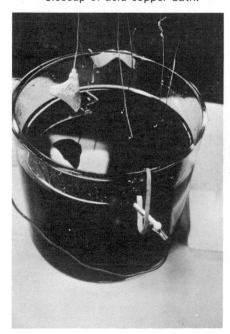

baths should be covered when not in use. Heat for the baths can be supplied by an aquarium-type immersion heater, which is glass enclosed and can be clamped to the side of the tank.

The electroforming operations can be broken down into two types: the deposition of metal onto a metallic matrix, and the deposition of metal onto non-metallic matrices.

Metallic matrices can be fabricated in many ways. Copper foil can be used as a basic matrix upon which to deposit silver. The foil can be bent, cut, and in other ways manipulated to achieve basic forms which are difficult to obtain by other methods.

The first step, in depositing metal on a metallic matrix, is to pass it through an electrocleaning bath. This is a proprietary alkaline detergent material which is placed in a stainless steel tank that acts as the anode, the matrix being the cathode. It is operated at about 6 volts, 180° F and the matrix is immersed in it for approximately 30 seconds. This step should not be omitted if an adherent deposit is desired. The matrix is then rinsed in water and placed into a silver strike solution for 30 seconds which further cleans the metal and deposits an adherent base coat of silver. This is a solution which has very little silver and a high cyanide concentration. The matrix is again the cathode, and the solution is in a stainless steel tank which acts as the anode. It is operated at 6 volts. After a water rinse, the matrix (cathode) finally goes into the silver electroforming bath, in which silver anodes are used in a glass tank. The voltage is approximately 1½ to 2 volts, and the matrix may remain in the solution for 15 minutes to 12 hours or longer, depending upon how thick the final deposit is to be. Most work can be accomplished in about 4 hours.

When depositing metal on a non-conductive surface, such as wax, styrofoam, wood, bone, plastic, or ceramic, the material must first be made electrically conductive. This is done by spraying or brushing on a conductive silver coating, available as a proprietary substance. After the conductive coating has been applied the piece is immersed in an acid copper solution to build up a thin protective coating of copper before immersion in the silver bath. This is done because silver is readily soluble in cyanide, and if this piece were first immersed in the silver-cyanide bath, the sprayed silver coating would be dissolved before silver could be deposited on it. After removal from the copper bath, the piece must be rinsed and then transferred to the silver electroforming bath, where the final silver coating is deposited.

When metal is deposited on a wax matrix, the wax can be melted out, leaving a thin hollow shell. It is also possible to use styrofoam as a matrix to be burned out.

The diagrams below show the processes by which metal is deposited onto the surface of the matrix to form the piece of jewelry.

ELECTROFORMING ON A NON-CONDUCTIVE MATRIX

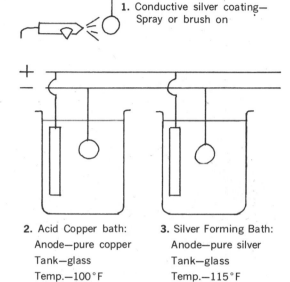

1. Conductive silver coating—
Spray or brush on

2. Acid Copper bath:
Anode—pure copper
Tank—glass
Temp.—100° F
Voltage—2v

3. Silver Forming Bath:
Anode—pure silver
Tank—glass
Temp.—115° F
Voltage—2v

To activate the transference of metal to the matrix an electrical current is required.

CURRENT FLOW DURING ELECTROFORMING

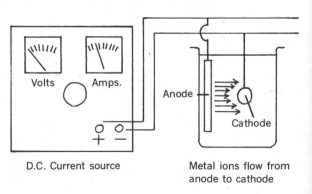

Volts Amps.

Anode

Cathode

D.C. Current source

Metal ions flow from anode to cathode

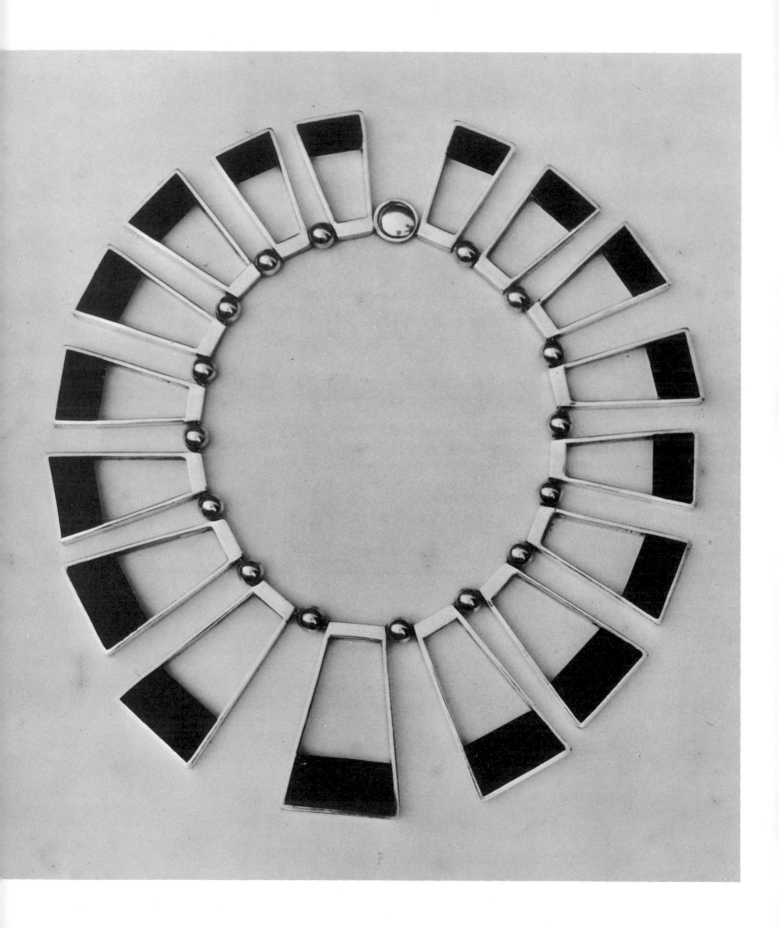

combined methods

Two or more of the many jewelry methods described throughout the book can be combined and various materials added to further enrich a surface, introduce a color, or include another element of design.

Combining methods and materials allows a wide latitude for the craftsman to use imagination and selection.

Some of the possibilities in combining methods and materials is forging used with sawed and pierced designs, repoussé with etched surfaces, metal inlaid with another material, forging and granulation with enameling, beads of ivory, amber, or lapis lazuli set into a cast piece, rosewood set into a forged piece, or porcelain imbedded in an electroformed piece.

A smoothly polished stone might be shown to advantage in a setting of roughly textured metal. The same stone can be given a totally different character if held in position by a ring of forged metal. It can be changed still further by being set in a band which has a great deal of pierced designs.

The texture and quality of wood can be heightened when surrounded by a smooth plane of silver or gold, or the already rich surface of granulation given another dimension when combined with enamels.

(Above) Gold earring with pearls, glass, and beryl variety emerald, Byzantine, 7th century A.D., found at Medina el Fayoum. Courtesy of The Cleveland Museum of Art.

(Left) Pin, cast in two sections, white gold with half round pearls, by Thomas Gentille. Photograph by Ferdinand Boesch

(Opposite page) Silver necklace combined with ebony and cocobolo wood inserts, by Arline Fisch. Courtesy of the American Craftsmen's Council. Photograph by Lynn Fayman's Studio.

Combining methods and materials presupposes a working knowledge of the techniques involved and the restraint necessary to select the correct balance between methods and materials, textures, and colors. In this the craftsman is guided by his own ingenuity and inventiveness. It is he who must decide in all instances which techniques should be combined, which grain or texture of wood will appear to the fullest advantage against a certain metal surface, or which stone will integrate best in a forged piece.

Included here and on the previous two pages is a portfolio of photographs which illustrate examples of jewelry made by combining methods.

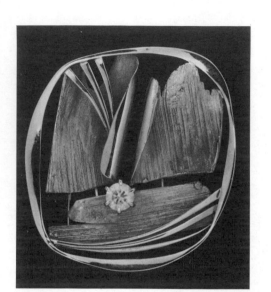

Pin, cast and forged, with faceted stone set in prongs, by Olaf Skoogfors. Courtesy of Craft Horizons.

Carved ivory armlet with copper inlay, Nigeria (Benin). Courtesy of The Museum of Primitive Art.

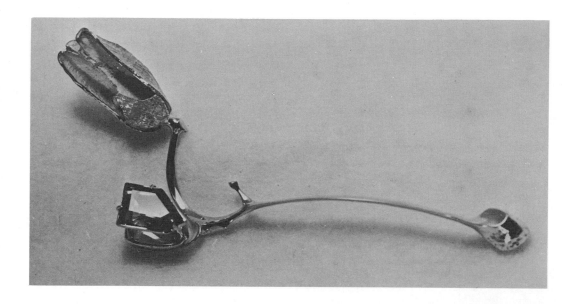

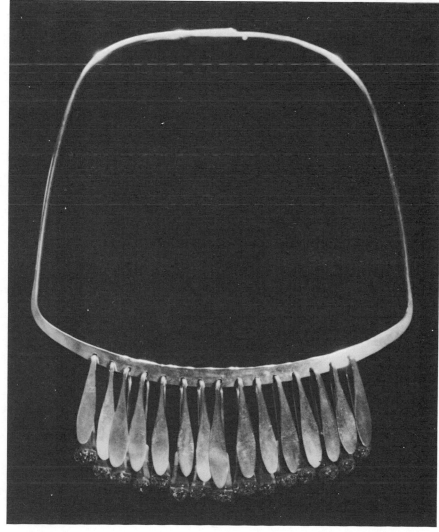

(Top) Pin with a citrine. Constructed of forged gold and cast weed pod, by Ruth Clark Radakovich. Courtesy of Craft Horizons.

(Center) Pendant of African blackwood (heartwood and sapwood) rimmed with silver, by Irving Potter. Courtesy of Craft Horizons. Photograph by James H. Karates.

(Right) Forged silver necklace with ceramic and glass stones. "Cascade", by Elsa Freund. Courtesy of Craft Horizons.

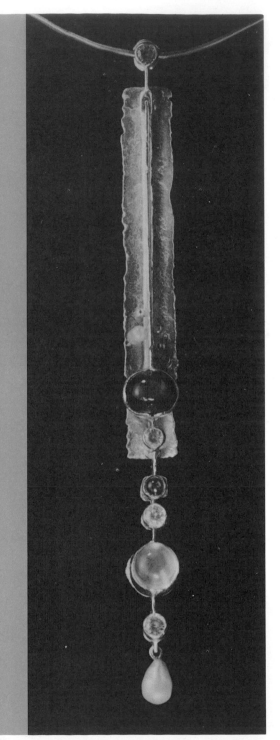

Gold pendant, combining ruby, moonstone, sapphire, pearl, and diamond, by Reinhold Reiling, Germany. Courtesy of Craft Horizons.

lapidary

Lapis is Latin for stone, and lapidary which is derived from it refers to the art of cutting and polishing gemstones, to the one who cuts and polishes them, and to the place where he works.

Man has always been fascinated with gems, with their romance, and with their beauty, and his use of them as good luck charms antedates recorded history. Even their names seem to weave spells—peridot, tourmaline, amethyst, bloodstone, moonstone, sardonyx, zircon, topaz, chalcedony, jasper, malachite, tiger eye, onyx, and carnelian.

Traditionally a number of minerals have been classified as to color, luster, durability, and rarity into two arbitrary categories, precious and semiprecious. Emeralds, rubies, sapphires, and diamonds have been considered to be precious, and all other gem minerals semiprecious.

At times, the opal has been included in the precious group but only when of superior quality, and although the pearl is not a mineral it, too, has been so classified. The pearl, one of the oldest known gems, is organic in origin, as are coral, jet, and amber.

Today, however, the distinction between precious and semiprecious stones is thought to be very slight because of the wide variation in quality available, and those terms are being used less and less. It is becoming more customary to use the term "gem stone," and any stone worth cutting and polishing is worthy of being so classified.

Friedrich Mohs, a German mineralogist, categorized stones and minerals as to their degrees of hardness or softness (the harder stone will scratch the softer). Mohs' scale has 10 degrees; talc, the softest known mineral, is at grade 1 on the scale, and diamond, the hardest known, at grade 10. The scale is fairly uniform through grades 1 to 9, but the difference in hardness between grades 9 and 10 is so much greater than that from 1 to 9 that the diamond is not truly represented. Its hardness is considerably greater than the ruby and sapphire at grade 9.

Gem stones are cut into two basic shapes, the cabochon and the facet. The cabochon, one of the oldest and simplest of cuts is the one most often tried first by the beginner. It is a dome shape, usually of an opaque or translucent stone, and may have a variety of geometric outlines. It is smooth-surfaced and ranges in size and shape from a low, round, flat-based cabochon to a high-domed oval double cabochon. Most cabochons are cut flat on the bottom, but the double ones have a domed surface on the bottom also.

Transparent gem stones are customarily cut and polished into facets or flat planes to increase their brilliance and to take advantage of their intrinsic ability to reflect and transmit light. Like the cabochon, a faceted stone may possess any geometrical shape. The facet should be made symmetrical and meet at a point and have no appearance of roundness. Opaque stones are sometimes also faceted.

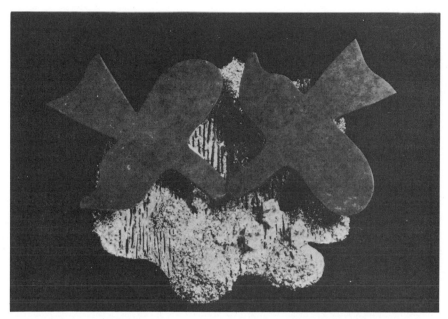

(Left) Pendant, "Head of a Woman" cut amethyst set in gold, Roman, Early Empire. Courtesy of The Cleveland Museum of Art

(Above) Gold pin with bird forms of lapis lazuli, and diamonds, "Pelias and Neleus", by Georges Braque. Courtesy of Craft Horizons.

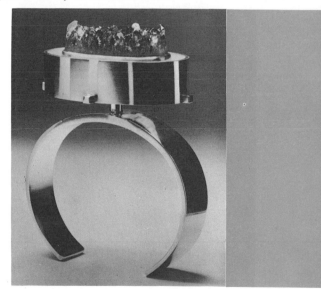

Silver ring with uncut amethyst quartz crystals, by Sigurd Persson, Sweden. Courtesy of Craft Horizons.

Earrings from Nepal, silver set with turquoise. Courtesy of The Museum of Contemporary Crafts. Photograph by Ferdinand Boesch.

White gold ring with amethyst—
Friedrich Becker, Germany

Lapidary is a precise and exact craft and, until the early years of this century, one that was exclusively guarded by those in the trade. The situation is quite different now, much information on cutting gem stones is available, and manufacturers are producing more lapidary equipment. For most purposes the craftsman can obtain stones already cut, but an elementary knowledge of lapidary can be helpful for the times when a particular size or shape of stone is necessary for a piece.

The beginner could also find a great deal of pleasure in collecting stones, and using them in a *rough* or *tumbled* state. These natural stones can also be purchased from dealers. Roughs are just what the name implies, uncut stones used in their natural state without cutting or polishing. The stones should, of course, have an attractive color and shape. An ideal way to secure the rough stones is to wrap them with round or square wires which can be bent or twisted around the stone to form various designs. Earrings can be very simply made in this manner.

Tumbled stones can also be wire wrapped. They are rough stones that are polished smooth by being rotated in a tumbling machine. The machine can be purchased or can be homemade using paint cans as the tumbling barrels. The barrels should contain an abrasive grit and tumble slowly for many hours until the stones are bright and smooth.

SOME STONE CUTS

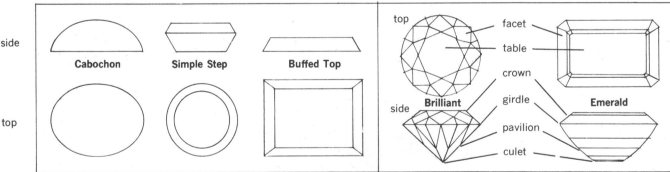

Pegging A Pearl

Pearls can be secured by pegs and pearl cement. A metal backing for the pearl is made, it should be smaller than the diameter of the pearl; a hole is drilled through its center; and a hole is drilled into the pearl. The peg, of square wire twisted, the same diameter as the base hole, is inserted into the hole and soldered at the back of the base; the base is then soldered to the jewelry piece. The cement is placed into the pearl hole; the pearl pressed over the peg; and the cement allowed to dry.

White gold ring with amethyst—
Friedrich Becker, Germany

Yellow gold ring with rose topaz—
Friedrich Becker, Germany

White gold ring with smoky citrine—
Sigurd Persson, Sweden

Cast pin in 18K yellow gold set with pearls, by Thomas
Gentille. Photograph by Ferdinand Boesch.

Pin in 18K white gold with pearls and inlaid clam shell,
by Thomas Gentille. Photograph by Ferdinand Boesch.

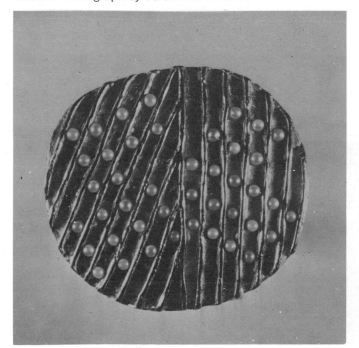

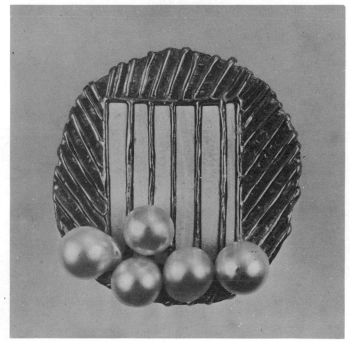

found objects

What most people would throw away—cracked pottery, torn photographs, watch gears and crystals, dime store jewelry, broken glass—when incorporated with metals can become the basis of found object jewelry. Pieces so made are imaginative, have eye appeal, and can be highly sophisticated.

The found objects can be crisscrossed, layered between metals, soldered together or onto a sheet metal background, or placed on fused wires and accented with a baroque pearl or any other gem stone.

Materials such as felt, papier mâché, nails, and heavy rope are other contemporary approaches to found object jewelry. In past cultures, seashell, tortoise shell, bone, ivory, beads, feathers, and dried grasses were fashioned into many fine personal and religious pieces of adornment, rich in texture and color.

I have given to students the project of making found object jewelry that would last for only one day. Some amazing pieces resulted—strands of black seaweed on a loosely woven vine evolved into a pendant necklace; moss and delicate weed pods glued onto bark became a pin; small silver-grey slices of driftwood were made into long elegant earrings; and a curved length of polished bone was fashioned into a dinner ring.

A number of these one-day pieces were seriously considered and were later translated into metal to become finished pieces. Objects do not necessarily have to be translated into conventional materials, bone can be carved, shell cut, string braided, and innumerable other natural materials can be used as they are.

The experimentation with construction and forms can be endless and the diversification of materials nearly limitless. The photographs illustrating this section show early and contemporary found object jewelry.

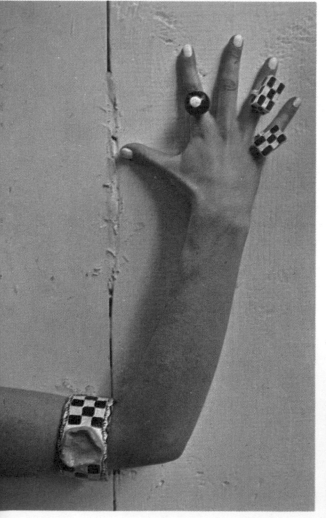

Arm bracelet and rings of painted papier mâché, by Ashlock Aubi. Courtesy of the American Craftsmen's Council.

Mexican bracelet with carved design on conch shell. Courtesy of The Museum of Primitive Art.

Pendant, turtle shell and fiber, Melanesia (Kap Kap). Courtesy of The Museum of Primitive Art. Photograph by Renita Hanfling.

Pendant necklace of fiber and metal, by L. F. Smith. Courtesy of the American Craftsmen's Council.

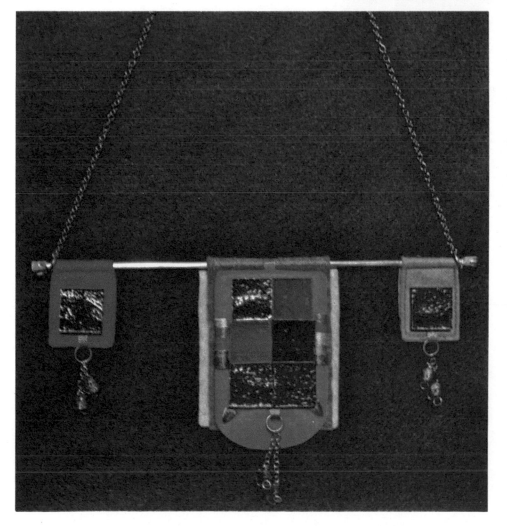

Arm band of straw, New Guinea Highlands, 1950. Courtesy of The University Museum, Philadelphia. Photograph by Renita Hanfling.

Collar of incised silver plates stitched on black velvet, by Arline Fisch. Courtesy of The Museum of Contemporary Crafts. Photograph by Renita Hanfling.

Arm band, Urubu Indian, upper Amazon, Brazil. Tropical feathers and seed beads. Courtesy of The Museum of the American Indian, Heye Foundation. Photograph by Renita Hanfling.

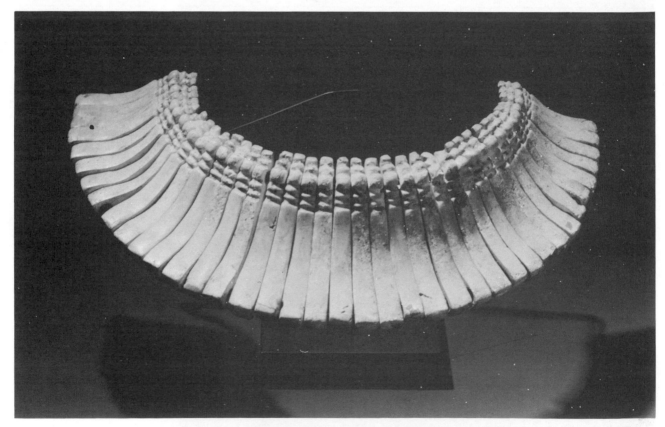

A collar of carved conch shell, Panama. Courtesy of The Museum of Primitive Art. Photograph by Charles Uht.

Necklace of pelican bone whistles with incised decoration, Teguala Indians, Panama. Courtesy of The Museum of the American Indian, Heye Foundation.

glossary

Acid solution (sulfuric acid and water)—Used during the pickling process to clean metal of fire scale and flux. Sparex #2, a non-corrosive pickling solution, can be substituted for sulfuric acid.

Acrylic—A synthetic transparent plastic compound used as a fixative.

Alloying—Fusing two or more metals together in a crucible until they are molten. Brass is an alloy of copper and zinc. Fine silver and fine gold are alloyed with base metals for extra hardness.

Annealing—Heating metal to a high temperature and cooling it quickly so that it becomes soft and malleable. (See p. 61).

Asphaltum—A brown or black varnish derived from petroleum, applied to metal as an acid resist during etching.

Carborundum stone—The trade name for a silicon carbide abrasive.

Casein—A yellow-white powder derived from milk, acts as an adhesive. Used in transferring designs to metal.

Chasing hammer—Broad, flat-faced hammer shaped with a long thin-necked handle for rapid hammering, drives chasing tools and other punches.

Crucible—A vessel made of refractory material such as clay or porcelain, for melting metals when a high degree of heat is required.

Debubblizer—A commercially prepared liquid solution applied to wax model during casting to avoid the formation of bubbles.

Ductile—Refers to those metals capable of being drawn into fine wire. One gram of fine silver can be drawn into a wire 3 miles long, and an ounce of fine gold drawn 35 miles long.

Electrodeposition—The depositing of electrically charged metals onto a desired surface or object (matrix).

Emery cloth, paper, stick—A coated abrasive used on metal to remove file marks and scratches.

Findings—Mechanical fastenings which hold jewelry in position while being worn.

Fine silver—Pure unalloyed silver, after gold the most malleable and ductile of metals. Too soft for most jewelry purposes, it is used mainly for bezels and as a base for enamels.

Fire scale—A copper oxide that forms on chemically unprotected metal during soldering. Prevented by fluxing and removed by pickling.

Flux—A commercial preparation containing borax, available in paste and liquid form. Checks fire scale, or oxides, during soldering and helps solder to flow by forming a protective film which keeps air away from the metal. Used also as an aid in melting metal in a crucible.

Gauge—Refers to the thickness of wire and sheet metal.

Gum tragacanth—A gum obtained from Asiatic trees, acts as a binder when applied in a water solution.

Karat—A term used to measure alloyed gold. The standards are based upon pure gold which has 24 karats; 18 K gold is 18 parts pure gold and 6 parts of another metal. Alloy golds may also be 22 K, 20 K, 14 K, 12 K, and 10 K. Those below 10 K cannot legally be stamped with a Karat mark. Not to be confused with carat which is a unit of weight for gem stones.

Kiln—A furnace or heated chamber lined with a refractory material, such as fire brick, in which high temperatures can be reached.

Iron binding wire—Soft, annealed iron wire used in binding metals for soldering. Available in all standard wire gauges.

Liver of sulfur (potassium sulfide)—Used during oxidation to color metals. Gives a bluish-black finish to silver and copper.

Malleable—The quality in metal which enables it to be hardened or stretched without cracking or breaking. Gold, the most malleable of all metals, can be hammered into semi-transparent sheets less than 1/300,000 of an inch thick.

Millimeter—A unit of measurement. 25.4 millimeters equals one inch.

Pitch—An ideal base or support for metal in engraving, chasing, and repoussé. Composed of pitch, plaster of Paris, and tallow, it is easy to apply and remove.

Pitch bowl (block)—A semi-spherical metal bowl filled with pitch. Supports work for engraving, repoussé, and chasing.

Pitch bowl pad—A leather ring or rubber pad which enables the bowl to be held at any desired angle.

Punch—A sharp pointed pick or awl. When hammered into metal makes a dent or hole for piercing.

RPM—Revolutions per minute.

Shellac stick—A round, flat-tapered stick for holding small work to be engraved.

Soldering equipment—Torch, annealing pan with lump pumice, charcoal block, and heating frame.

Tripoli (buffing compound)—A fast cutting abrasive for removing scratches from metal.

Vise—Useful for holding stakes or work being filed or sawed. Clamps to workbench.

suppliers

General:

C. W. Somers & Company
387 Washington Street
Boston, Mass. 02108

Alexander Saunders & Co., Inc.
28 Chestnut Street (Route 9D)
Cold Spring, N.Y. 10516

Allcraft Tool & Supply Co., Inc.
215 Park Avenue
Hicksville, N.Y. 11801

Anchor Tool & Supply Co., Inc.
12 John Street
New York, N.Y. 10038

Oceanside Gem Imports, Inc.
P.O. Box 222
426 Marion Street
Oceanside, N.Y. 11572

T. B. Hagstoz & Son
709 Sansom Street
Philadelphia, Pa. 19106

John A. Ischantre
7 N. Liberty Street
Baltimore, Md. 21201

C. R. Hill Company
35 W. Grand River Avenue
Detroit, Mich. 48226

Swartchild E. Company
22 W. Madison Street
Chicago, Ill. 60602

Thomas C. Thompson Co., Dept CH
1539 Old Deerfield Road
Highland Park, Ill. 60035

Southwest Smelting & Refining Co.
P.O. Box 2010
1708 Jackson Street
Dallas, Texas 75221

Jewelry Distributing Company
315 West 5th Street
Los Angeles, Calif. 90013

Grieger's, Inc.
Dept 20
1633 East Walnut Street
Pasadena, Calif. 91106

Gems Galore
1328 El Camino Real
Mt. View, Calif. 94040

Enamels:

Kraft Korner
5842½ Mayfield Road
Cleveland, Ohio 44124

Norbert L. Cochran
2540 South Fletcher Ave.
Fernandina Beach, Fla. 32034

Gem Stones:

William J. Orkin, Inc.
373 Washington Street
Boston, Mass. 02108

Francis Hoover
12445 Chandler Blvd.
No. Hollywood, Calif. 91607

S. Schweitzer & Co.
Dept H, P.O. Box 71
Gedney Station
White Plains, N.Y. 10605

Ernest W. Beissinger
402 Clark Building
Pittsburgh, Pa. 15222

John Barry Company
Dept C, P.O. Box 15
Detroit, Mich. 48231

Roy F. Clifton
3100 Terrace Drive
Kokomo, Ind. 46901

Flexible Shaft Machine:

The Foredom Electric Co.
Bethel, Conn. 06801

bibliography

BOOKS:

BATES, Kenneth F. *Enameling Principles and Practice.*
The World Publishing Company, Cleveland and New York, 1951,
2nd Edition.

BAXTER, William T. L. *Jewelry, Gem Cutting and Metalcraft.* McGraw Hill Book Company, Inc., New York, 1950,
3rd Edition.

BOVIN, Murray. *Jewelry Making for Schools, Tradesmen, and Craftsmen.* Murray Bovin, 68–36 108th St., Forest Hills,
Long Island, N.Y., 1964.

HOFFMAN, Herbert, and DAVIDSON, Patricia F. *Greek Gold, Jewelry from the Age of Alexander.* Museum of Fine Arts,
Boston, The Brooklyn Museum, Brooklyn, N.Y., Virginia Museum
of Fine Arts, Richmond, 1966.

LEWES, Klares. *Jewelry Making for the Amateur,* Reinhold
Publishing Corp., New York, 1965.

NEUMANN, Robert von. *The Design and Creation of Jewelry.* Chilton Company, Philadelphia and New York, 1961

SPERISEN, Francis J. *The Art of the Lapidary.* The Bruce
Publishing Co., Milwaukee, 1961, Revised Edition.

WINEBRENNER, Kenneth D. *Jewelry Making, as an art expression.* International Textbook Co., 1953.

MAGAZINES:

Craft Horizons 16 East 52nd St., New York. A bimonthly
magazine published by the American Craftsmen's Council

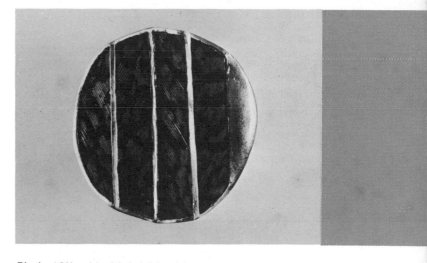

Pin in 18K gold with inlaid golden pheasant feathers, by
Thomas Gentille. Photograph by Ferdinand Boesch.

Color photographs on back cover by Renita Hanfling.

The following list is of professional schools, universities, and workshops that offer courses in the jewelry craft. Most of the schools listed operate on a year round basis—for further information, write to the school direct.

Arizona State University
Dept. of Art
Tempe, **Arizona** 85281

University of Arkansas
Fayetteville, **Arkansas** 72701

Arkansas Arts Center
MacArthur Park
Little Rock, **Arkansas** 72203

University of Southern California
Idyllwild School of Music and the Arts
Idyllwild, **California** 92349

Barnsdall Art & Craft Center
4800 Hollywood Blvd.
Los Angeles, **California** 90027

Mendocino Art Center
Box 36
Mendocino, **California** 95460

Richmond Art Center
Civic Center Plaza
Richmond, **California** 94804

Sacramento State College
6000 Jay Street
Sacramento, **California** 95819

University of the Pacific
Stockton, **California** 95204

Western State College
Art Dept.
Gunnison, **Colorado** 81230

Brookfield Craft Center, Inc.
Brookfield, **Connecticut** 06804

Eastern Connecticut State College
Willimantic, **Connecticut** 06226

Berry College
Mount Berry, **Georgia** 30149

Western Illinois University
Macomb, **Illinois** 61455

Indiana University
Fine Arts Dept.
Bloomington, **Indiana** 47401

Herron School of Art
of Indiana University
1701 No. Pennsylvania St.
Indianapolis, **Indiana** 46202

Ball State University
Art Dept.
Muncie, **Indiana** 47306

Des Moines Art Center
Greenwood Park
Des Moines, **Iowa** 50312

Wichita Art Association, Inc.
9112 East Central
Wichita, **Kansas** 67206

Berea College
Art Dept.
Berea, **Kentucky** 40403

Haystack Mountain School of Crafts
Deer Isle, **Maine** 04627

School of the Museum of Fine Arts
230 The Fenway
Boston, **Massachusetts** 02115

Workshops in Creative Arts
Boston YWCA
140 Clarendon Street
Boston, **Massachusetts** 02116

Craft Center
25 Sagamore Road
Worchester, **Massachusetts** 01650

Bloomfield Art Association
1516 So. Cranbrook Road
Birmingham, **Michigan** 48009

Cranbrook Academy of Art
500 Lone Pine Road
Bloomfield Hills, **Michigan** 48013

University of Minnesota
Dept. of Art
Duluth, **Minnesota** 55816

Essayons Studio, Inc.
8725 Big Bend Blvd.
St. Louis, **Missouri** 63119

Kearny State College
School of Business & Technology
Industrial Education Dept.
Kearny, **Nebraska** 68847

Sharon Arts Center, Inc.
RFD 2
Peterborough, **New Hampshire** 03458

Adult Program
Great Neck Public Schools
10 Arrandale Avenue
Great Neck, **New York** 11024

Crafts Students League
West Side YWCA
840 8th Avenue
New York, **New York** 10019

Westchester Art Workshop
County Center Building
White Plains, **New York** 10607

Woodstock Guild of Craftsmen
34 Tinker Street
Woodstock, **New York** 12498

Penland School of Crafts
Penland, **North Carolina** 28765

Arts & Crafts Association
610 Coliseum Drive
Winston-Salem, **North Carolina** 27106

Bowling Green State University
School of Art
Bowling Green, **Ohio** 43402

The Cleveland Institute of Art
11141 East Blvd.
Cleveland, **Ohio** 44106

Kent State University
School of Art
Kent, **Ohio** 44242

Temple University
Tyler School of Art
Beech & Penrose Avenues
Philadelphia, **Pennsylvania** 19126

Arrowmont School of Arts & Crafts
P.O. Box 567
Gatlinburg, **Tennessee** 37738

Memphis Academy of Arts
Overton Park
Memphis, **Tennessee** 38112

Museum of Fine Arts, Houston
School of Art
1001 Bissonnet
Houston, **Texas** 77005

Fletcher Farm Craft School
Ludlow, **Vermont** 05149

Bellevue Community College
3000 140th Place Southeast
Bellevue, **Washington** 98007

Oglebay Institute, Downtown Center
841½ National Road
Wheeling, **West Virginia** 26003

Canada:

New Brunswick School of Arts & Crafts
Fundy National Park
Alma, New Brunswick, **Canada**

Canadian Guild of Crafts
2025 Peel Street
Montreal, Quebec, **Canada**